This book is by a practitioner who really believes in what he advocates. Not only does he believe in it—he does it! The book is full of practical advice, useful tips and valuable insights for training leaders. But what makes the book most special is that it takes us through 2 Timothy and, using this key part of the Bible's own leadership training school, inspires the reader to get training future leaders. I recommend it highly.

— WILLIAM TAYLOR, RECTOR ST HELEN'S BISHOPSGATE AND CHAIRMAN OF RENEW

I love this book! It's a book which needs reading many times to ensure its divine wisdom, Biblical teaching and relevant practice is received. I have known Paul as a Gospel colleague and good friend since his arrival in Sheffield; his personal humility and Godly passion jump out from the pages of this excellent book. It will, I believe, make a significant contribution not only to the vital ministry of training leaders, but also to raising up Biblical disciples. Thank you Paul!

— REVD CANON MICK WOODHEAD, TEAM RECTOR, STC SHEFFIELD

This is a brilliant book for those searching for a resource to train future leaders. It is full of razor sharp teaching on 2 Timothy and is crammed with insightful applications. It will provide all of us with a clear and workable strategy for the training of more gospel ministers. Get this book if you want to intentionally and practically raise up new leaders.

— LEE MCMUNN, MISSION DIRECTOR, ANGLICAN MISSION IN ENGLAND (AMIE)

This is a beautifully clear and compelling look at the Bible's own 'manual' for faithfully training leaders who are loyal to the gospel. Paul Williams draws on years of experience to illustrate and apply apostolic teaching on this crucial subject. If you want to get serious about handing on the baton to the next generation, this is a great place to start!

— LEE GATISS, DIRECTOR OF CHURCH SOCIETY, CHAIRMAN OF THE JUNIOR ANGLICAN EVANGELICAL CONFERENCE (JAEC), AND EDITOR OF *REACH, BUILD, SEND: A PATTERN FOR ANGLICAN MINISTRY.*

A month's worth of tasty short chapters savouring the apostle Paul's training priorities and patterns of ministry from 2 Timothy. From start to finish Paul Williams shares his own ups and downs in learning to apply apostolic training priorities today with a welcome realism and humility, and a strong plea to renew our commitment to a vital task.

— JOHNNY JUCKES, PRESIDENT OF OAK
HILL COLLEGE, LONDON

Too many church leaders do not make the vital task of developing faithful future leaders a priority in their ministry. Paul Williams has written this little book based on a thorough grasp of 2 Timothy in order to address this. It is easy to read and comes in a wisdom-like format of 30 short chapters. It is an excellent resource which will provide an existing leader with a practical framework for actually getting on with doing what we are in danger of only paying lip service to.

— MARK BURKILL, PAST CHAIRMAN OF
REFORM

TRAINING LEADERS

HOW TO ENSURE GOSPEL SUCCESSION FOR THE NEXT GENERATION

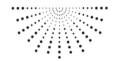

PAUL WILLIAMS

EP Books (Evangelical Press), Registered Office: 140 Coniscliffe Road, Darlington, Co Durham DL3 7RT

admin@epbooks.org

www.epbooks.org

EP Books are distributed in the USA by:

JPL Books, order@jplbooks.com www.jplbooks.com

100fthose USA, www.100fthose.com sales.us@100fthose.com

British Library Cataloguing in Publication Data available

Print ISBN 978-1-78397-289-0

eBook ISBN 978-1-78397-290-6

In loving memory of David and Richard and with thanks to Wallace. Three men who trained me in gospel ministry.

CONTENTS

Introduction: The priority of priorities   xi

1. The priority of training leaders   1
2. Train leaders by doing life with them   9
3. Train leaders to rely upon the Lord   15
4. Train leaders to suffer for the gospel   22
5. Train leaders the authentic gospel for which they   27
   must suffer
6. Train leaders how to guard the gospel   36
7. Train leaders to expect desertion, but to rejoice in   41
   faithfulness
8. Train leaders on the job   45
9. Train leaders to train leaders   50
10. Train leaders to be sacrificial and hardworking   53
11. Train leaders to focus on Christ who suffered and   60
    was glorified
12. Train leaders to be careful with words   66
13. Train leaders to work hard in the Word   71
14. Train leaders to avoid playing around with dodgy   75
    theology
15. Train leaders to believe in the doctrine of God's   79
    elect
16. Train leaders to understand the good that comes   82
    from false teaching in the church
17. Train leaders not to be quarrelsome   85
18. Train leaders to know the times we live in   90
19. Train leaders to have nothing to do with certain   95
    people
20. Train leaders to follow those who are godly under   99
    pressure

21. Train leaders never to depart from the Scriptures   104

22. Train leaders to believe the Bible will fully equip   109
     them for ministry

23. Train leaders to preach the Word   113

24. Train leaders to do the work of the evangelist   122

25. Train leaders to carry out every ministry duty   128

26. Train leaders to evaluate ministry in the light of   131
     the end

27. Train leaders by being vulnerable with them   135

28. Train leaders to read books   139

29. Train leaders about Christian assurance   143

30. Train leaders   149

     Notes   155

INTRODUCTION: THE PRIORITY OF PRIORITIES

66 Unless you make training leaders a priority you'll never do it.

I had been asked to address a group of pastors on the importance of evangelism in the local church. The staff team I was part of at the time agreed to give me their best thoughts on the subject. Helpful comments and godly wisdom were tumbling out of their mouths at a rate that left my wrist aching from scribbling furiously on my note pad. They were on a roll; it was one of those moments that reminded me what a joy it is to be part of a dynamic team of committed Christian workers. What's more, my presentation would be considerably improved! Then, with the room positively buzzing with ideas, one comment silenced the lot of us. 'Unless you make evangelism a priority you'll never do it.' Sheena's offering flew across the table in a sentence containing the words 'unless' and 'never.' Sheena was not bombastic or dogmatic or overbearing. She was not one for hyperbolic overstatements. She was measured, gentle, considered and wise. With Sheena you got the impression that every word had been carefully chosen. Yet here was an assertive declaration that left no room for manoeuvre. With all eyes now firmly fixed in Sheena's direction, she elaborated, 'The church family will knock on your door asking for your help through a pastoral crisis, or to lead their Bible study, or to chair another meeting, but you will never have unbelievers knocking on your door asking you how to become a Christian. So unless you make evangelism a priority you'll never do it.'

Of course, what is true of evangelism is true of almost anything. There are so many demands in Christian leadership that unless we are very clear what we must do above everything else we'll find essentials swamped by the immediate and urgent needs of the day. Without clear priorities we'll be influenced by who shouts loudest and we'll feel the pressure to respond to the desires of those we fear the most.

Barely a day goes by when I don't ask myself, 'How am I going to get everything done today?' Most Sunday evenings I am full of heartfelt gratitude to God that I've made it through the week. On Monday morning, when I look at the week ahead, I find myself praying a genuine prayer of desperation about the demands of the next seven days. So on Sunday evening, as I walk through my front door, still standing despite all the demands of the past week, I have a sense of thankful relief: 'I made it. Thank you Lord.'

On the rare occasions when the week ahead looks reasonably manageable, and I'm lured into the optimistic hope that I might even start to tackle that lengthy list of long-neglected tasks, invariably something crops up to dash my hopeful aspirations. I can be super-organised, very disciplined and incredibly efficient with my time (by saying 'I can,' please understand that I mean, in theory, I can!). I can have a clear understanding of my priorities. I can be stubbornly rigid in sticking to them. And still I can have my plans disrupted by the demands of pastoral ministry.

Ten days before Easter I had carefully worked out how I would arrive at Maundy Thursday prepared and ready for such an important and demanding weekend. Then at 10.15pm on Tuesday evening of that week, when I was just about to turn in for the night, the ping of a text message alerted me to a request to go to the hospital. An elderly member of the church family was dying. Of course I went. In the days that followed, my diary was consumed by that pastoral 'crisis.' Then came the funeral, in Holy Week of all weeks, which was already about as full as I thought I could cope with.

I cite *that* incident, but the thing is, I didn't have to scratch around to think of an example of an important pastoral demand coming at an 'inconvenient' time. I could fill pages with examples of exactly that sort of thing because it happens all the time. There are always people knocking on my door (metaphorically and sometimes literally) asking for my help. In any normal week I find myself overwhelmed with all that has to be done. Then on top of that, the unexpected crashes in to my world.

My point is simple and reasserts Sheena's comment—gospel ministry is demanding. Time is limited. There is always more to be done. So, unless we have clear priorities and then make our priorities a priority, they'll easily be squeezed out. Unless we're clear and convinced what our priorities should be, we're toast.

I left theological college with very clear priorities: Bible teaching, evangelism, prayer, pastoral care. Or three 'P's' if you will, proclamation, prayer and people. From my first day in paid gospel ministry I ordered my diary around those things. The mornings would be given to prayer and preparation, afternoons to visiting people. Unbelievers interested in the gospel would always get my attention first, barring a genuine pastoral crisis. Other things, even important things and urgent things, would have to wait. All well and good, but there was something missing from my list of priorities. The glaring omission? Training. It doesn't begin with 'P' so it was never going to fit neatly into my alliterative list of priorities. But seriously, where was training as a priority? More specifically where did the training of the next generation of gospel workers fit into my schedule? And even more specifically, training the next generation of church leaders. I could argue that I was training every time I taught the Bible, and that is true (or at least it should be). But what about deliberately identifying, selecting, and then investing in the training of individuals to be Christian leaders? Ask me back then if I thought it was important and I think I'd have said it was. But was it important enough for me to make it a priority? I confess that in those early years, training leaders was far enough down my 'to do' list to result in me never getting around to it. Training leaders was another great idea that got buried under a pile of good intentions.

My guess is, I'm not the only one. Ask many Christian leaders who they are deliberately training to be future church leaders and they might talk about training in general terms. Push them further about being more targeted in the task of training leaders and they might bemoan the fact that they don't have any suitable candidates. They might even respond with a weary and heavy heart, 'don't you understand how busy I am?'

You, on the other hand, may be one of those who has made

training the next generation of gospel workers a prime concern. Brilliant. But, perhaps you're like me. Even when I did begin to make training leaders a priority, I did not have a clear strategy. You may well feel as if you're 'making it up as you go along.' At the risk of sounding patronising, let me commend you for at least having a go. When something is important it is better to improvise and throw something together on the fly than not do it at all. Besides, you're probably doing a better job than you realise. But that said, even better than winging it, would be to have a clear, defined and proven strategy; a training course if you will. Better still, imagine getting your hands on an inspired and infallible approach to training leaders. The good news is, you have. I'm not referring to this book (that really would be a ridiculously pompous and outrageous claim and enough to persuade you to immediately send this book to a charity shop!). No, the book I refer to is Paul's second letter to Timothy. It is my conviction that in this letter God has given us a training manual. As we see how Paul trained Timothy we have a paradigm to equip us to train leaders. It is also my conviction that Paul's charge to Timothy to train leaders, is a charge laid on every gospel minister.

From chapter 2 of this book we'll walk through the book of 2 Timothy and watch how Paul trained Timothy in gospel ministry. That, I believe, will give something of a blueprint for training all future gospel workers.

Of course, 2 Timothy is not the only Bible material given to us to equip us to train future leaders. First Timothy, Titus and Matthew's gospel all immediately spring to mind as Bible books that equip us to train others. So 2 Timothy is not a comprehensive training manual, but I hope to convince you it's a great place to start.

But before we begin our walk through the letter, we must first be persuaded that training the next generation of leaders is a priority we must adopt. So that's where we will begin. Seeking the conviction that training the next generation of gospel workers must be a prime concern of ours. Because unless you make training leaders a priority you'll never do it.

THE PRIORITY OF TRAINING LEADERS

> Do you want to spend the rest of your life selling sugared water, or do you want to come with me and change the world?

— STEVE JOBS

> For I am already being poured out like a drink offering, and the time for my departure is near.

— 2 TIMOTHY 4:6

Steven Paul Jobs was the chairman, chief executive officer, and co-founder of Apple. Apple needs no introduction from me. Virtually everyone on the planet has heard of the tech giant. Apple is one of only a handful of companies that is so famous it is identified worldwide simply by its logo. Even as I mention it, I imagine you can see, in your mind's eye, the apple with a bite taken out of it. Apple is the world's richest company posting the largest *quarterly* profits of all time. At the end of 2018, Apple made $20.1bn (£14bn) in three months!

Steve Jobs tried to lure executive John Sculley to work for Apple and to leave Pepsi (another global brand). Jobs famously asked Sculley, 'Do you want to spend the rest of your life selling sugared water, or do you want to come with me and change the world?' Through Apple products, Jobs wanted to change the way communication happened between everyone on the planet —and arguably he achieved that aim. But more than that, Steve Jobs wanted to ensure that the technological revolution continued beyond his death. Or rather, he wanted to ensure that Apple continued to lead the way in this digital revolution. Chris Green, commenting on Jobs' biography writes:

> Jobs ... notably relaxes at two points in the narrative: once when he appoints the designer Jonny Ive, a man with the same aesthetic and love of detail, and again when he appoints Tim Cook, someone who shares his view of manufacturing and products.[1]

Reading that was a massive rebuke to me. Jobs may not have been selling sugary water but, when all's said and done, he was still only selling tech devices. Jobs may well have changed global communication, but in the gospel we have the message that changes eternity. Yet how many of us prepares for our death by ensuring succession, with the precision, care and passion that Jobs did?

Being a pastor I have had the enormous privilege of sitting with people as they die. It is one of the hardest things I have to do, and in many ways I don't care to ever have to do it again. It's heart-wrenching watching the physical suffering, seeing the psychological struggle, hearing the theological questioning, and witnessing the emotional agony of loving relationships being torn apart. That said, it is also a huge privilege to be there in those 'sacred' moments.

Approaching death, people have trusted me enough to share with me their deepest reflections. Often they've given me a frank assessment of their entire life. Revealing to me their regrets, their disappointments, the things they wish they'd done differently. Yes, I also hear the joys, successes and happy memories of their life too, usually when they're reminiscing with loved ones in my presence. But on the whole, it's the mistakes and regrets they share with me, because they want to 'confess,' 'repent,' or simply confide in someone who they hope won't condemn them. Having been in that honoured position on a good number of occasions has made me reflect on my own final days. I've imagined myself talking to a pastor sitting next to *my* deathbed. There'll be huge things for me to confess. Even as a forgiven Christian, I long for a giant eraser to rub out chapters that largely remain buried deep in the canyons of my mind. I wish I could turn the clock back and re-run some episodes of my soap opera. I'd love to rewrite those horrible smudges that blot the pages of my life's story. I imagine you feel the same. And now that I've led you onto the hallowed turf of the end of your life, allow me to narrow the search considerably. As you lay on your deathbed, how will you assess your *gospel ministry*? In so many ways it's a very unhelpful question that forces an artificial compartmentalisation of life. It's not helpful to draw a wedge between ministry and the rest of life. It's unhelpful because we can't claim to have had a 'good ministry' if we've been morally wayward, or neglected the family, or repeatedly exhibited a dodgy character trait in our 'private life.' Yet, let me ask you the question all the same, 'What constitutes a faithful ministry?'

When Paul wrote his second letter to Timothy he was about to die. His time on earth was almost up. He was writing from prison believing his death was imminent: 'For I am already being poured out like a drink offering, and the time for my departure is near' (2 Timothy 4:6).

As Paul faced up to the prospect of being catapulted into eternity at any moment, this is how he assessed his life:

> I have fought the good fight, I have finished the race, I have kept the faith. Now there is in store for me the crown of righteousness, which the Lord, the righteous Judge, will award to me on that day—and not only to me, but also to all who have longed for his appearing.
>
> — 2 TIMOTHY 4:7-8

Paul has total confidence in the gospel of forgiveness in Christ that made him right with God and ensured an eternal prize way beyond anything we experience here on earth. He knew that all his mistakes had been wiped clean. And let's face it, the great apostle had a serious criminal record. A record of rebellion against God and his people that was more than a smudge on the odd page of his story. A significant chapter of his life was devoted to a bloody crusade against Christians. He led the campaign. Hunting Christians down in order to exterminate them and eliminate every trace of their Way from the planet. Yet Paul knew that in the gospel there was complete pardon. More than that, there was in store for him a 'crown of righteousness' (2 Timothy 4:8). Paul could face death with confidence because of the glorious gospel of Jesus Christ.

But note Paul's assessment of his life: 'I have fought the

good fight, I have finished the race, I have kept the faith' (2 Timothy 4:7).

Those famous last words of Paul raise the question, 'What must life and ministry need to consist of to be able to confidently join Paul in saying verse 7?'

To answer that question, I might look back through chapter 4. If I've preached the Word faithfully, in season and out of season (verse 2); endured hardship and done the work of the evangelist (verse 5); discharged all the duties of ministry (verse 5); then surely I could claim to have lived my life well? The great apostle had lived this way. He'd preached the Word in season and out of season, when it suited him and when it didn't, when it was convenient and when it wasn't, when it would be received well and when it wouldn't. He'd endured hardship. When Paul entered a new town he didn't ask, 'What are the hotels like in this town?' but, 'What are the prisons like here?' (Acts 20:23). He'd done the work of the evangelist—boy, had he done the work of the evangelist! He travelled all over the known world planting churches and sharing Jesus Christ with anyone who would listen, and those who wouldn't. Paul had lived all this. But there was something more. Something more that enabled him to say at the end of his life, 'I have fought the good fight, I have finished the race, I have kept the faith.' Paul had trained the next generation of gospel workers. He accomplished for the gospel cause what Steve Jobs did for Apple. He'd recruited, and in Paul's case trained, those who would continue the great mission to change eternity. Paul had Timothy in place to succeed him. And training future gospel workers is a significant element to a faithful ministry.

That's a big statement, so allow me to lay out three ways to substantiate that claim.

First, consider the language in verse 7: 'I have fought the

good fight, I have finished the race, I have kept the faith' (2 Timothy 4:7). As we read verse 7 it should remind us of Paul's words in chapter 2:3-6. 'I have fought the good fight' (2 Timothy 4:7) is the picture of the trooper from 2 Timothy 2:4: 'No one serving as a soldier gets entangled in civilian affairs, but rather tries to please his commanding officer.' 'I have finished the race' (2 Timothy 4:7) is the language of the runner, reminding us of 2 Timothy 2:5, 'anyone who competes as an athlete does not receive the victor's crown except by competing according to the rules.' As Paul writes chapter 4:7, he deliberately uses the same imagery and metaphors that take us back to the beginning of chapter 2, a chapter all about training the next generation of gospel leaders: 'And the things you have heard me say in the presence of many witnesses entrust to reliable people who will also be qualified to teach others' (2 Timothy 2:2).

We'll look at that verse in more detail when we get to chapter 9 of this book, but for now, very simply, the image of the relay race asserts the imperative that the baton of the gospel is put firmly into the hands of the next generation of gospel leaders. It's crucial to pass on the gospel to people who will in turn pass on the gospel baton to the next generation of church leaders. That's the way to ensure that gospel ministry continues beyond the death of any Christian leader.

In short, the words in chapter 4 smack of the leadership training and gospel succession of chapter 2. Paul had personally 'fought the good fight' and he had 'run the race' but that 'fighting' and 'running' involved training Timothy (and others) in Christian leadership.

Second, consider the last phrase in verse 7: 'I have kept the faith' (2 Timothy 4:7). John Stott writes:

> This may conceivably mean 'I have kept faith

with my Master.' But in the context of this letter, which emphasises so strongly the importance of guarding the deposit of revealed truth, it is more likely that Paul is affirming his faithfulness in this respect. 'I have safely preserved, as a guardian or steward, the gospel treasure committed to my trust.'[2]

This is the point about guarding and keeping the gospel in 2 Timothy: we guard the gospel by giving it away. We'll see this when we look at 2 Timothy 1:14 in chapter 6 of this book. There we'll see that guarding the gospel is supremely done as we give the gospel to people who will themselves faithfully pass on the gospel to other leaders. Right through 2 Timothy we'll see how Paul kept the faith by training Timothy in the content of the gospel and telling Timothy to be someone who passed it on to others. Paul 'kept the faith' by training Timothy (and others).

The third reason I'm convinced that Paul was confident that he'd been faithful in ministry because he'd trained others, comes from the immediate context in chapter 4. Paul's words in chapter 4:7 follow his great charge to Timothy. The charge that began: 'In the presence of God and of Christ Jesus, who will judge the living and the dead, and in view of his appearing and his kingdom, I give you this charge: Preach the word' (2 Timothy 4:1-2).

We'll look at these remarkably powerful words in detail in chapter 23 but for now, simply note how Paul charged Timothy to be uncompromising in gospel leadership. This charge is Paul handing on the baton to Timothy.

So then, both the language in chapter 4:7 and the immediate context is about training and handing on the task of leadership to the next generation of gospel leaders. All that convinces me that Paul's ministry was faithful because it included training the next generation of Christian leaders. In Timothy, Paul has a reliable man who would in turn, train other gospel workers to train yet more Christian leaders. Paul has put in place a pattern that will guard the gospel by ensuring that the gospel will be reliably passed on for generations to come.

The challenge for us is to incorporate training the next generation of gospel workers into our ministry. To fail to do so is to fall short in a significant aspect of Christian leadership. The gospel is not a gospel of works, so our salvation is not dependent on how many people we've trained. But as with any deathbed experience, we can know we're saved and still have regrets. Embracing lessons from 2 Timothy will save us from looking back at the end of our lives and lamenting that we didn't make a priority of training others.

This letter should convince us to make leadership training a priority. But it also equips us for the task. It is an infallible and inspired manual to train leaders. So where do we start?

TRAIN LEADERS BY DOING LIFE
WITH THEM

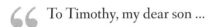 To Timothy, my dear son ...

— 2 TIMOTHY 1:2

I'm very grateful for people who've trained me through my life. For my long suffering teachers at secondary school who kept labouring away with a lad who wasn't interested in anything beyond playing sport. For my piano teacher who put up with someone who didn't practice from one week to the next. For my football coach who never stopped encouraging me even though he was working with the unrealistic dreams of a footballing numpty who wanted to play for Leeds United.

It is not the fault of those who invested in me that I only achieved 5 O-levels, can't play the piano and didn't even manage to play in the Isthmian League for Letchworth Garden City FC. Those who trained me tried their best.

But there are two people who trained me quite differently to the way my school teachers, piano tutor and football coach trained me, and that's my parents. Like the others, they too stuck with someone who was a lazy good-for-nothing most of the time and rarely grateful for all their efforts. But because Christine and Jack Williams were my parents, they trained me quite differently to anyone else in my life. They knew me and loved me at a level that was more personal than anyone else. As a result their training was more perfectly tailored for *me* than any other training I received in any other sphere of life. What's more, their training saw them share their lives with me (it's an obvious point, but it's important to log it all the same). Living with them for the first 18 years of my life, I observed their way of life (without me even realising all that I was taking in at the time). I saw how they responded to difficulties, their approach to money, their decision-making process, how they used their time, what made them tick. At first-hand I experienced their parenting skills and techniques.

At the same time, by living in close quarters, Mum and Dad saw me as I really was. They saw my highs and lows. Subsequently they knew what motivated me and they knew what would never spur me on. They knew my weaknesses and my failings. They knew me so well that I couldn't pretend with them. Of course at times I did try to pull the wool over their eyes, but the only person I was fooling was myself. The point is, they knew me so well, they knew exactly the training I needed for life. And while they trained me, I picked up a whole host of life skills from simply being around them.

When it comes to training the next generation of gospel workers, Paul gives us a model that is more like the personal investment of a parent, than the professional instruction of a professor. He begins his letter to Timothy, 'To Timothy, my dear son ...' (2 Timothy 1:2).

It's the same in 1 Timothy; Paul addresses Timothy as his son. As we read on we are left in no doubt that this is not a formal designation; Paul really was like a father to Timothy. Subsequently, the way he trained Timothy was so much more than a business transaction. Timothy wasn't another student attending a theological training course for future gospel ministers. Paul shared his life and ministry with Timothy; he opened himself up to the young man. Paul got to know Timothy and Paul allowed Timothy to get to know him. Paul loved Timothy and as a result Timothy grew to love Paul. These opening verses express the depth of that love.

See first that Paul's commitment and care for Timothy was expressed in him praying for Timothy: 'I thank God, whom I serve, as my ancestors did, with a clear conscience, as night and day I constantly remember you in my prayers' (2 Timothy 1:3). Night and day: constant prayer.

What we pray about reflects what really matters to us. How *much* we pray about what we pray about further reveals our love, passion and concern for what really matters to us. Barely a day goes by when I don't pray for my wife, my three children and my brother and his family. Those are the people that I care for above everyone else on this planet. Here is Paul, praying for Timothy, every day, throughout the day, and even night and day. Prayer is a crucial starting point when it comes to training gospel workers. Praying regularly for those we are encouraging towards church leadership is a must. How often we pray for them probably indicates the depth of our relationship to them and almost certainly reveals our level of commitment to them.

Second, in Paul's prayer we see Paul's attitude towards Timothy. His prayer was full of thankfulness for Timothy (verse 3). This is the great apostle, a man who was revered and respected, one who had experienced the most astonishing revelations of God and from God (2 Corinthians 12:1-5), one through whom God would give a huge proportion of the foundation documents on which the entire church of Jesus Christ would be built. Yet Paul was thankful for Timothy. Paul didn't think to himself, 'How lucky Timothy is to have me as his mentor.' On the contrary, Paul was thankful to God for Timothy. What a humble attitude. Be sure, it will not go well in training leaders if we have an over-inflated view of ourselves.

For a year I was put on placement with a church leader who was exceptionally able. He was gifted in understanding the Bible with a razor-sharp clarity and great insight. Yet, sadly, he was very full of himself. I was grateful for the time he gave to instruct me to be a better Bible teacher, but not once did he leave me with the impression that he was thankful to have me around. It was quite different for Timothy with Paul. Here is Paul stating his thankfulness to God for Timothy.

Thirdly, Paul's love and concern for Timothy was expressed in a deep desire to be with Timothy and to support him: 'Recalling your tears, I long to see you, so that I may be filled with joy' (2 Timothy 1:4).

At some point Timothy had wept with Paul. Perhaps it was the time when Paul said goodbye to the Ephesian elders in Miletus (Acts 20:37). That said, in the next chapter I'll offer another suggestion for Timothy's tears. For now, whatever Paul's referring to, it's quite something when you're so comfortable with a 'supervisor' that you can break down in front of them. That will only happen in a secure, trusted and open relationship.

And that heartfelt love and concern was mutual. Paul was so fond of the young man that recalling Timothy's tears broke Paul's heart. He wanted to see Timothy again. Just being with Timothy would be enough to bring Paul joy. This is such a rebuke to me. Too often in gospel ministry I want to keep my distance, put up my guard, project an image of self-sufficient strength and competence. That's not good in ministry and it's certainly not good when training others.

John Piper has written a book entitled *Brothers, We Are Not Professionals.* In it, Piper doesn't encourage sloppy 'unprofessionalism' in gospel ministry; his point is that Pastors are not to adopt a business model when it comes to ministry. In that sense we are not professionals, we are not CEOs, we are family. That's clearly Paul's approach to training Timothy. Timothy was so precious to Paul that to see Timothy would fill Paul with joy. 'I long to see you, so that I may be filled with joy' (2 Timothy 1:4). Paul enjoyed knowing Timothy. He enjoyed his company. He loved him so much he wanted to know he was OK.

Sadly, I have to offer a word of caution here. We live at a time when mentors have misused their positions of authority. The dangers of sexual and spiritual abuse are rightly being exposed. When training others we must be sure not to take advantage of those in our care. We should put in place carefully considered guidelines to ensure that everyone is protected. But, while it may feel like walking a relational tightrope at times, we must not be so withdrawn that we lose the huge value of sharing life.

Fourthly, Paul knew all about Timothy's family: 'I am reminded of your sincere faith, which first lived in your grandmother Lois and in your mother Eunice' (2 Timothy 1:5).

If you want to know how well you know someone, ask yourself what you know about their loved ones. My first training incumbent, David Wheaton, regularly asked me about my extended family. It was never a mere formality. David was genuinely interested in what my family were up to. David and his wife Joy invited my parents to lunch whenever they were in town. David and Joy knew what was going on in the lives of the people that mattered to me.

Fifthly, and crucially, Paul knew the sincerity of Timothy's faith in Jesus Christ (verse 5). A sincere faith is the first thing we should look for when selecting who to train for gospel leadership. There has to be more than sincerity of faith, but there mustn't be less. It seems obvious, and yet we can easily slip into looking for other things first. In a youth worker we might look for someone who's trendy. We might be wowed by a children's worker who has an ability with puppets. We might employ an associate pastor because of their brilliant theological perception and superbly crafted sermons. Nothing is wrong with any of those things, but first and foremost we must look for a sincere faith. Not just faith in Christ, but a sincere faith in Christ. How can we perceive sincerity of faith? Only when we know someone really well. Paul knew Timothy in an appropriately intimate way.

In many ways these opening verses tell us much about Timothy. But they also tell us much about Paul and the way he trained people for gospel ministry. He gave heart and soul (love and prayer) to Timothy. He invested himself in Timothy. He opened himself up to Timothy. He loved Timothy. To Paul, Timothy was not a project, he was a son.

3

TRAIN LEADERS TO RELY UPON
THE LORD

> For this reason I remind you to fan into flame the
> gift of God, which is in you through the laying on
> of my hands. For the Spirit God gave us does not
> make us timid, but gives us power, love and self-
> discipline.

— 2 TIMOTHY 1:6-7

E very year a group of people join our ministry trainee
scheme to explore whether full-time paid gospel ministry
is for them. The scheme gives a taste of gospel ministry from the
inside. Most of our trainees are post-grads, straight out of
university. Straight off we warn them that it'll be hard work.
Halfway through the first term we expect them to be tired-out.
Nothing surprising so far, because most people moving out of
full-time education and into any kind of full-time work find it a
demanding step up. But a few years back we had a GP join the
ministry trainee scheme. She was in her thirties, a hardworking
lass and a gifted evangelist. In a review at the end of the first

term she said to me, 'I have never worked so hard in my life.' I found that impossible to believe. So we explored together what she had found so demanding. We talked about the long hours, but as a GP she was used to that. There was the volume of work to do, but that wasn't anything new to her. We thought about the need to keep so many plates spinning, and that feeling that the work is never done. But having a ton of different things on the go and always more patients to see had been her experience in general practice for many years. We discussed how demanding people were, but she was a GP for goodness sake.

Why did a hardworking GP find the first 13 weeks of a gospel trainee year so demanding? As we systematically considered everything, we came down to the fact that, on top of all of the above, there are the spiritual pressures of the job. We're in a spiritual battle; in gospel ministry we're dealing with the most important issues anyone could possible consider. There is nothing more important than the issue of eternity: is it to be spent in heaven or hell? Knowing that the stakes are so high means that it really matters when Christians fail, Christians fall out, and we encounter 'Christian' false teaching. Gospel ministry matters more than anything else in the world. That's a pressure we can't escape. Maybe it's that pressure that sees so many Christian leaders struggle to go the distance.

As we read 2 Timothy we discover the struggles Timothy was encountering as a Christian leader. We've already been given a hint about Timothy's state of mind. Timothy, a grown man, has been in tears (2 Timothy 1:4). Paul wants to see Timothy to support him, but Paul is in prison, so he wrote this letter to encourage Timothy to keep going amidst all the struggles of gospel ministry. Where does that encouragement start? Paul reminds Timothy of the work of the indwelling Holy Spirit:

For this reason I remind you to fan into flame the gift of God, which is in you through the laying on of my hands. For the Spirit God gave us does not make us timid, but gives us power, love and self-discipline.

— 2 TIMOTHY 1:6-7

Much has been written about these verses. Because this is not a commentary I'll leave you to read the differing views. I'm taking it that the gift given to Timothy was, as Alfred Plummer suggests, 'the authority and power to be a minister of Christ.'[1]

The authority came from the moment Paul (and quite possibly others) laid hands on Timothy to commission him into leadership and church oversight. That's certainly what the laying on of hands was about in Acts 13:3. Timothy was given the authority to be the leader of the church in Ephesus. Now, Paul is encouraging Timothy to go for it, to be the leader he's been appointed to be. He reminds Timothy that he was considered to be the right man for the job: 'Timothy, at the laying on of my hands you were given the authority to be a church leader.' But this is not just a matter of 'take the lead, pull up your socks, try harder and go for it.' Paul also assures Timothy of the power which equips us for gospel ministry, the precious Holy Spirit (verse 7).

As we've already considered there are many pressures in church leadership. Every year I meet up with a group of friends from my days at theological college. We have an annual 24 hours together to try and keep each other accountable, to pray for each other and to spur each other on. At our last meeting, one of my friends said, 'I have five more years before I retire. I love preaching and telling people about Jesus, but I am exhausted and worn down by all the rubbish.' He went on to tell us the sort of rubbish that drags him down. Bickering in the church family; moral failures; lack of forgiveness between Christians; petty church politics; battles against false teaching.

The rubbish is so trying. It grinds us down to the point where we wonder if we can keep going in Christian leadership. And the truth is that while *we* can't keep going, *the Holy Spirit* can keep us going. That's Paul's point here. We have been given the Holy Spirit. He will equip us and empower us to keep at it.

Please, don't mishear me at this point. I don't want to be heard to be suggesting that people who give up are not relying upon the Holy Spirit and are trying to do everything in their own strength. Pastoral issues are complex and obviously I don't know the particular details of why individuals have needed to step out of full-time paid gospel ministry. But even bearing in mind all the pastoral complexities, and in a real desire to avoid sounding trite and superficial, what an encouragement it is to be reminded that God has equipped us for the task. He has given us his invaluable presence and power in the person of the Holy Spirit. That surely has to be one of the first things we must tell those we're training. 'You've been given the Holy Spirit to equip you for ministry. You can't do it on your own. There will be tough times ahead. Times when you'll feel as if you can't go on any longer. Times when you'll be reduced to tears. In those times, remember the Spirit within you.'

Remember what the Holy Spirit does for us: 'For the Spirit God gave us does not make us timid, but gives us power, love and self-discipline' (2 Timothy 1:7). Just as there's much debate about verse 6, much has been written about verse 7. This verse is often expounded to suggest that Timothy's natural character was rather spineless. The argument goes that he was a shy retiring boy, Timid Timothy. I'm not convinced that's right at all. But for now, even if that is right then this verse is saying 'The Holy Spirit gives the power, the love and the self-discipline to be what we should be in pastoral ministry.' In other words, 'God equips.'

Now if that's how to read this verse, then it is a rebuke to us when we consider some people unsuitable for ministry because of their natural persona. That way of thinking doesn't allow for the work of the Holy Spirit to equip people. Indeed, isn't it the case that God delights in using the weak to demonstrate his strength (1 Corinthians 1:27-29; 2 Corinthians 12:9). God has always delighted to take weak people to be the leaders of his people, so that all the glory goes to God himself. So if the 'Timid Tim' thesis *is* how we should understand verse 7, then it tells us that we must not rule out of gospel ministry those who are shy or hesitant, or not naturally good 'up front.' Gloriously I have seen God take people who at first sight are not obvious candidates for gospel ministry, and make them into exceptional leaders in God's church. The Holy Spirit gives power, love and self-discipline for the task of leading God's people.

All that said, I think verse 7 is saying something different. I don't buy the line that Paul is writing to a timid lad who wouldn't say boo to a goose. That doesn't square with everything we know about Timothy. Think of the gospel ministry Paul and Timothy had together—Paul often called for Timothy to join him to be his right-hand man. He regularly sent Timothy off into the hardest and most challenging gospel situations. Timothy travelled all over the world without any of our modern day communications to hand—the modes of transport that make world travel so straightforward these days weren't available to Timothy. Yet Timothy trudged all over the Mediterranean, walking into dangerous situations to support Paul in gospel ministry.

The evidence in the New Testament doesn't support the thought that Timothy was a timid boy. Rather, try this for size: Timothy had been worn down by the pressures of ministry. In this letter we read about the twin problems of false teachers and disloyalty. During Timothy's annual accountability review, with tears in his eyes, he might well have said to Paul, 'I love preaching and telling people about Jesus, but I am exhausted and worn down by all the rubbish; the rubbish of fighting false teaching and the rubbish of Christians who I thought were friends, stabbing me in the back.' So Timothy's temptation is to stop fighting against false teaching. He's tempted to go into his shell. The normal battles of ministry have worn him down. But the thing is, the rubbish is part and parcel of normal gospel ministry. And if he's going to be a faithful gospel leader, he has to keep fighting for the truth.

Allow me to be autobiographical for a moment. The denomination I'm involved in is badly infected by false teaching. It's such a desperate situation that I sometimes wonder how long I can remain in the denomination without feeling completely compromised. The constant battle against false teaching wears me out. I simply want to get on with proclaiming the gospel to unbelievers and building up Christians in the faith. But I'm regularly distracted from that glorious gospel ministry because of significant theological error which has serious pastoral and eternal consequences. It's a time consuming and exhausting battle. So I'm tempted to keep my head down, get on with the job in the local church, which is largely a joy, and not engage with theological error in the wider church. In that sense I am timid when it comes to fighting against false teaching. I want to step away from battling against false teaching. I am tempted to timidly avoid that kind of engagement. But I doubt anyone who knows me would describe me as a person of timid disposition!

Here then is Timothy. A strong and capable leader, who has been worn down in the battle against false teaching and discouraged by the disappointment of disloyalty. It may have been those issues that reduced Timothy to tears. So, right at the beginning of this letter, it's as if Paul says to Timothy, 'I understand that you might feel like giving up the fight, but remember you have been given authority to hold your position and you have been given the Holy Spirit to equip you for the task. God did not give you a spirit of timidity, God gave you the Holy Spirit. He is the Spirit of power; he will give you the power to keep going in the battle and to stand up for the truth. He is the Spirit of love; he will help you to love God and love others enough to keep battling for the truth. He is the Spirit of self-discipline; when you feel like giving up, the Holy Spirit will enable you to pick yourself up and dust yourself down and keep going against all the false teaching and disloyalty that so discourages you.'

There's much we need to do when training future gospel leaders. But right up there is the need to remind 'trainees' how God equips for the task. He has given the Holy Spirit and he expects us to rely upon his Spirit. God doesn't expect us to do his work without him. The Holy Spirit is God himself, giving us all we need to keep going. And my, how we'll need his help.

4

TRAIN LEADERS TO SUFFER FOR THE GOSPEL

66 ... do not be ashamed of the testimony about our Lord or of me his prisoner. Rather, join with me in suffering for the gospel, by the power of God.

— 2 TIMOTHY 1:8

I'm not one for watching 'reality TV,' not least of all because it often seems to bear little resemblance to reality! But I have been fascinated by a couple of episodes of *SAS: Who Dares Wins*. In it, five ex-Special Forces soldiers recreate the SAS's secret selection process and put 30 people through their paces in the ultimate test of physical and psychological resilience. I know that I wouldn't last more than about five minutes under that kind of pressure. I am neither physically nor psychologically tough enough. So you won't be surprised to hear me say that I'm quite pleased that at theological college there wasn't an equivalent test to see if prospective pastors could endure suffering. But there needs to be, because authentic gospel ministry always involves suffering.

We'll read later in 2 Timothy that 'everyone who wants to live a godly life in Christ Jesus will be persecuted' (2 Timothy 3:12). Live a godly life and persecution and suffering will follow. Suffering comes with the territory of godly Christian living and it certainly comes in spades for leaders who live godly lives. People need to know that, when considering full-time paid gospel ministry. That said, I don't actually think that theological college syllabuses should include the pastoral equivalent of an SAS endurance test, although one book I read described how church leaders in China are taught at Bible college to escape from prison and scale vertical drops without hurting themselves, because, in that part of the world, incarceration is considered to come with the territory of gospel leadership!

But still I'm not advocating that theological colleges in the West try to do the same because the suffering I'm thinking about can't be reconstructed in a theological college. In 2 Timothy we discover how Paul had suffered the devastating pain of friends deserting the gospel and disowning him. The agony of that experience can only be 'felt' in the real world. It can't be reconstructed. That's one reason why training future gospel workers has to be done 'on the job' and not solely in the classroom, but more of that in chapter 8.

We've already read about Timothy's tears (2 Timothy 1:4). We don't know what caused such upset, but it might well have been the result of the false teachers and deserters he'd encountered. Whatever it was that caused him such distress, he needs to know that suffering is part and parcel of gospel ministry. That's what Paul does here.

Verses 8 to 12 are the brackets that form a section about suffering for the gospel. Note the repetition of the phrases: verse 8: 'Do not be ashamed.' Verse 12: 'I am not ashamed' (ESV).

Verse 8: 'Join with me in suffering for the gospel.' Verse 12: 'that is why I am suffering.'

Sometimes, remaining faithful to the gospel will result in suffering. And because faithful gospel ministry results in suffering we will be tempted to be ashamed of the gospel. After all, who wants to suffer? So Paul writes: 'do not be ashamed of the testimony about our Lord or of me his prisoner. Rather, join with me in suffering for the gospel, by the power of God' (2 Timothy 1:8).

Paul was suffering in prison just because he proclaimed the gospel. When that's a possibility, there's a temptation to either keep quiet about the gospel or to subtly change the gospel we proclaim.

Imagine yourself chatting with unbelieving friends. The conversation turns to Jesus. Your friends not only listen but show real interest in knowing more. So you tell them the good news of Jesus' death and resurrection. They're gripped by what you say and they ask you what happens to those who don't put their trust in Jesus. And this is the precise moment where you're tempted to be ashamed of the gospel. You know that conversations about eternal punishment always feel awkward. What's more you know some of your friends have already lost loved ones who weren't Christians. So, you assume that if you tell them about the eternal destiny of those who don't repent and believe, you're going to suffer for it. It is at this point that you need to hear Paul say, 'do not be ashamed of the testimony about our Lord ... Rather, join with me in suffering for the gospel' (2 Timothy 1:8).

It's brilliant being a Christian. There are many joys in following Christ, but it also includes declaring things that aren't fashionable. The gospel is counter-cultural. Faithful gospel ministry involves speaking out against the popular beliefs and values of the day. Being a Christian will mean being misunderstood and marginalised and persecuted. Even in Britain we can know a degree of religious oppression, so anyone who's ever talked to their friends about Jesus knows the temptation to be ashamed of the gospel, the urge to keep quiet about the hard and contentious parts of the glorious gospel of Jesus Christ.

Timothy would have known that temptation, so Paul taught Timothy that gospel ministry is a suffering ministry. But crucially, at the end of verse 8, Paul also taught Timothy that we can endure that suffering by the power of God: 'do not be ashamed of the testimony about our Lord or of me his prisoner. Rather, join with me in suffering for the gospel, by the power of God' (2 Timothy 1:8).

Here we see how verses 8 and 9 link to verses 6 and 7. In the last chapter we saw how Paul assured Timothy that he had been given the Holy Spirit, the Spirit of *power,* love and self-control. Now, here in the very next verse, Paul tells Timothy to stand up for the gospel by the *power* of God. The Holy Spirit is given precisely to empower us to endure suffering. It would be very easy to skip through this, not to ignore it, but at the same time not to emphasise it. It's crucial that we train gospel workers that they will suffer for the gospel, but it's vital that in the very next breath we explain that the Holy Spirit will equip us and empower us, in and through suffering.

I was talking to a newly ordained minister recently, a fine young man. He's a year out of college and loving the opportunities he has to teach Christians and proclaim the gospel to unbelievers. But with just one year in the job he said to me, 'Until I started I had no idea how many struggles and difficulties I'd encounter.' He went on, 'Graham [an older Christian who encouraged him into gospel ministry] told me it would be hard, but until you encounter it first-hand you can't know the extent of it.' Hearing that, I thought to myself, 'Well done Graham.' This young man had been taught that it would be hard. That didn't make it any easier, but now that he was encountering hardship he wasn't left wondering if he was doing something wrong. And he wasn't left saying, 'No-one ever told me it would be like this' or 'If I'd known this was what it involved I'd have never gone into church leadership.'

We must train people that gospel ministry is a suffering ministry. But in the very same breath we must tell them that God gives his Holy Spirit to empower us to endure suffering. If we don't teach people about the equipping of the Spirit, who in their right mind is going to go into gospel ministry?

Suffering for the gospel is an essential element of gospel ministry. But we're equipped for the task. The thing is, we must be sure that when we do suffer, it really is for the gospel that we suffer. That's the next thing Paul teaches Timothy.

5

TRAIN LEADERS THE AUTHENTIC GOSPEL FOR WHICH THEY MUST SUFFER

> And of this gospel I was appointed a herald and an apostle and a teacher.
>
> — 2 TIMOTHY 1:11

It's very easy to be persecuted. Be obnoxious. Be objectionable. Be unkind. Be a pain in the neck and you'll soon find yourself marginalised and ostracised. And there's the problem—what we sometimes class as Christian persecution, is actually suffering for being an unpleasant person.

Many years back someone said to me 'I love what you stand for, but I don't like the way you stand for it.' At the time it was painful to hear, but I'm extremely grateful for the man who had the courage to say it to me. His challenge helped me see that the way I 'stood up for the gospel' made it very hard for my detractors to hear what I was actually saying. Consequently, what I perceived as being shunned for the gospel, was in fact people sidelining me because I was being unattractive and objectionable.

In the last chapter we saw that gospel ministry is a suffering ministry, but we must be sure that we suffer for the gospel and not because we're insufferable. We've seen how 1 Timothy 1 verses 8 and 12 form a section in which Paul instructs Timothy not to be ashamed of the gospel even though he'll suffer for it. In verses 9 and 10 Paul then states the content of the authentic gospel. We can see that from verse 11 where he concludes, 'And of this gospel I was appointed a herald and an apostle and a teacher.' So, what we read in verses 9 and 10 is a summary of the authentic, apostolic gospel. It is this gospel that we must not deviate from. It is this gospel we must proclaim unashamedly. And it is this gospel that we are to suffer for:

> He has saved us and called us to a holy life—not because of anything we have done but because of his own purpose and grace. This grace was given us in Christ Jesus before the beginning of time, but it has now been revealed through the appearing of our Saviour, Christ Jesus, who has destroyed death and has brought life and immortality to light through the gospel.
>
> — 2 TIMOTHY 1:9-10

We must not assume that future leaders know and will teach the authentic, apostolic gospel. I rejoice to see young Christians of university age being taught all sorts of important Christian truth, things like the importance of having our identity in Christ and how to engage with culture. But I am concerned that those same young Christians are not being taught the fundamentals of the Christian gospel.

Some years ago I heard someone explain the danger of not explicitly teaching and emphasising the essential truths of the gospel in this way: 'The first generation teach the gospel, the second generation assumes the gospel and the third generation forgets the gospel.' The truth of that is evident in a number of national and international organisations that were established with clear gospel convictions and set up with clear Christian aims. Today, however, while many have (or had) 'Christian' in their title, they are not organisations that stand on or proclaim the gospel any longer. They are now only well-meaning philanthropic institutions.

It is because of this danger that Paul is reminding Timothy of the gospel, which he must not be ashamed of, and for which he will suffer. The section is a reminder to us that we must never assume that people know the gospel. We must teach the gospel to the next generation of church leaders. The moment we assume that people know the gospel, we are only one generation away from the gospel being forgotten.

By teaching the gospel I don't mean explaining a simple evangelistic outline, although it is invaluable to equip Christians with that kind of tool for ministry. A considered reading of 2 Timothy 1:9-10 shows that the gospel is much more than a few key truths to present to an enquirer. 'Paul's gospel' is full of deep theological truth that we must teach future church leaders.

So let's take a closer look at this gospel and as we do we will discover the rich theology that we'd do well to have as part of our training of future Christian leaders.

1. THE GOSPEL OF GRACE

> He has saved us and called us to a holy life—not because of anything we have done but because of his own purpose and grace. This grace was given us in Christ Jesus before the beginning of time.
>
> — 2 TIMOTHY 1:9

Paul presented election and predestination as part of the gospel of grace: 'This grace was given us in Christ Jesus before the beginning of time.' The gospel is God's initiative and is not earned or merited: 'not because of anything we have done.' The gospel of grace is about being 'in Christ.'

2. THE GOSPEL THAT SANCTIFIES

> He has saved us and called us to a holy life.
>
> — 2 TIMOTHY 1:9

The gospel when properly taught and understood transforms people. It results in a changed lifestyle. Yes, we are saved by the free grace of God, but Jesus calls us to deny self and take up our cross. Grace is free but it isn't cheap. The Bible knows nothing of a gospel that doesn't result in transformed lives.

3. THE GOSPEL OF REVELATION

> ... it has now been revealed ...
>
> — 2 TIMOTHY 1:10

The gospel isn't something that intelligent people work out for themselves. The gospel is revealed and supremely, it is revealed through the appearing of Jesus Christ. Jesus is the full and perfect revelation of God and the subject of the gospel.

4. THE GOSPEL OF SALVATION

> ... [the gospel] has now been revealed through the appearing of our *Saviour*, [italics mine] Christ Jesus, who has destroyed death ...
>
> — 2 TIMOTHY 1:10

The gospel is about being saved. We need a Saviour to save us from something. The gospel is about being saved from sin, death and judgement.

5. THE GOSPEL ABOUT ETERNITY

> Christ Jesus, who has destroyed death and has brought life and immortality to light through the gospel.

— 2 TIMOTHY 1:10

The gospel is about more than this life. Eternal life and immortality are at stake.

6. THE GOSPEL OF THE CROSS

❝ ... our Saviour ... who destroyed death ...

— 2 TIMOTHY 1:10

At the cross Jesus saved us and defeated death.

7. THE GOSPEL OF RESURRECTION

❝ Christ Jesus, who destroyed death and has brought life and immortality to light ...

— 2 TIMOTHY 1:10

It was through Jesus rising from the dead that death was defeated and life and immortality are proven to be possible for all who trust in Christ.

I doubt any of this is new to you. Indeed, it's the sort of list you may well have skim read because you already know all this stuff, but let me ask you to slow down at this point. If you're someone who highlights books, put your marker pen through those seven points above. Paul is stating clearly what the gospel is. These are the doctrines we must teach future church leaders:

sin, death, cross, resurrection, eternity, election, revelation, salvation, sanctification, resurrection, grace. This is the gospel that we must teach future gospel workers. This is the gospel that is to be proclaimed. This is the gospel that leaders must not deviate from ('do not be ashamed'). This is the gospel that we must suffer for: 'And of this gospel I was appointed a herald and an apostle and a teacher. That is why I am suffering as I am. Yet this is no cause for shame [ESV: But I am not ashamed]' (2 Timothy 1:11-12).

This is not a definitive summary of the gospel. There are many other 'summaries of the gospel' in the New Testament and they don't all contain the same points. I commend to you Allan Chapple's work in chapter 2 of his excellent book *True Devotion* where he 'harmonises' New Testament gospel summaries and demonstrates what is essential to be faithful to the revealed gospel. What we can see from verse 8 is that the gospel and suffering for the gospel comes when we speak about Jesus and when we align ourselves with Paul: 'do not be ashamed of the testimony about our Lord or of me his prisoner. Rather, join with me in suffering for the gospel, by the power of God' (2 Timothy 1:8).

For Paul, the gospel is not *just* a set of propositional truths. It's not merely a set of doctrines. The gospel is personal, in that it is about a person:

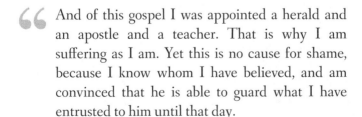

And of this gospel I was appointed a herald and an apostle and a teacher. That is why I am suffering as I am. Yet this is no cause for shame, because I know whom I have believed, and am convinced that he is able to guard what I have entrusted to him until that day.

— 2 TIMOTHY 1:11-12

Paul knows 'whom' he has believed, not 'what' he has believed. For many years, even though I was really converted, and even though I was in Christian leadership, I think the gospel for me was about a set of doctrinal statements and not primarily about the person of Jesus. It sounds terrible when I put it like that. For Paul the gospel was about Jesus. There is a significant difference because knowing '*whom* I have believed' and not 'what I have believed' (verse 12).

Allan Chapple expresses this brilliantly. See the endnote for a fuller explanation of his point. Chapple writes:

> We have nothing to offer the world except Jesus—and he is also what the church needs all the time. This is what distinguishes the gospel from an ideology. Christian preaching and teaching is more than setting out theological ideas we want our hearers to embrace. The truth we declare is the vehicle by which the Lord himself comes to us. Yes, people must receive and hold fast to the truth—but this means much more than committing to a particular doctrinal framework or worldview. By proclaiming the word of truth, we are inviting the world to meet a glorious person.[1]

Of course, 'the faith' in the New Testament *is* a way of talking about a body of teaching, but 'the faith' teaches us about Jesus and points us to Jesus. 'The faith' is about him. When we have this clear we suffer for *Christ*, the person who 'loved me and gave himself up for me' and not simply for a body of belief. That changes everything. It gives me a different motivation to suffer and will go a long way to ensuring that I suffer for Jesus and his gospel and not because I'm a pompous big head who rails against those who do not share my doctrine.

6

TRAIN LEADERS HOW TO GUARD THE GOSPEL

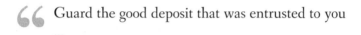 Guard the good deposit that was entrusted to you ...

— 2 TIMOTHY 1:14

One of the abiding memories from my childhood is seeing my Mum and Dad all dressed up and ready to go out for the evening. I think it sticks in my mind because it was such an infrequent event. I was raised in a loving, working class family, on a safe council estate. I grew up surrounded by decent hardworking people. My parents were people of principle and wholesome values. My brother and I never went without but Mum and Dad were never flush with money. As a result they didn't go out very often. I can think of only a handful of times when they were 'dressed up to the nines.' That's probably why that image of them all 'dolled up' is such a vivid one for me.

I can still see Dad in his best suit, shoes glinting from being highly polished. And there was Mum. Hair done, wearing a little, 'tastefully applied' make-up, and elegant in her best frock. Around her neck lay a pearl necklace. It's that piece of jewellery that gives me reason to recount this memory to you. As I recall it was an heirloom. Not valuable enough to retire on you understand (Mum and Dad came from modest family backgrounds), but it would have been one of the more valuable things my hardworking parents owned, not to mention the sentimental value. In that sense it was priceless. It looked stunning around Mum's neck, but she hardly ever wore it. In part because Mum and Dad didn't go out very often and neither of them were the flashy type, but primarily because it was so valuable to Mum. Subsequently that necklace didn't often see the light of day. Most of the time it was tucked away somewhere safe, buried somewhere in a drawer in my parents' bedroom, kept out of sight so that it would never be stolen. Mum guarded that pearl necklace by keeping it hidden away. Well that's what you do when you have something valuable isn't it? You guard it, by hiding it away somewhere safe, don't you? Not if it's the gospel you don't.

That is why I am suffering as I am. Yet this is no cause for shame, because I know whom I have believed, and am convinced that he is able to guard what I have entrusted to him until that day.

What you heard from me, keep as the pattern of sound teaching, with faith and love in Christ Jesus. Guard the good deposit that was entrusted to you—guard it with the help of the Holy Spirit who lives in us.

— 2 TIMOTHY 1:12-14

Paul tells Timothy to guard something here. That something is the gospel of grace that he's been speaking of in the previous verses, the pattern of sound teaching about Jesus. The gospel is so precious it has to be guarded. It is after all the way we are saved (2 Timothy 1:9) for all eternity. It could hardly be more precious. But the way we guard the gospel is two-fold.

First, we must not change the gospel. In the previous chapter we saw how Paul clearly laid out the gospel of grace that we must be prepared to suffer for. Now Paul clearly states, 'What you heard from me, keep as the pattern of sound teaching' (2 Timothy 1:12).

It is because we'll suffer for the gospel that we'll be tempted to change it, but we have no right to meddle with it. It's not ours to change. It has come from God, 'revealed through the appearing of our Saviour, Christ Jesus' (2 Timothy 1:10). It has been entrusted to us (2 Timothy 1:14). So we are to guard it by not changing it when we're tempted to be ashamed of it.

Second, we guard the gospel by giving it away. Here's the surprise. It's what Paul has been talking about in the preceding verses. Don't be ashamed of the gospel. Be ready to suffer for the gospel. Keep telling the gospel—give it away. It's so counter-intuitive; anything else we own that's really precious, we guard by holding on to it. Keeping it under lock and key or buried under a pile of cardigans in a bedroom drawer. We tuck it away from people who might steal it. But we guard the gospel by giving it away, passing it on as it actually is. We do that in evangelism. But in this context, when it comes to training leaders, we guard the gospel by ensuring that future leaders know the authentic apostolic gospel. We must give it to people who are convinced that they must not change it and who in turn will give it away to others, who will not tamper with it but who in turn will pass it on. Here we see clearly why training the next generation of gospel leaders will enable us to say at the end of our lives, 'I have fought the good fight, finished the race, and *kept the faith*' (2 Timothy 4:7, emphasis mine). Paul kept the faith by giving it away to people who will not alter it and will be sure to pass it on, unadulterated, to others who will do the same.

To guard the gospel is an awesome responsibility. But a word of encouragement, it's not all down to us. Paul reminds Timothy that God himself will guard his precious gospel: 'Guard the good deposit that was entrusted to you—guard it with the help of the Holy Spirit who lives in us' (2 Timothy 1:14).

John Stott writes:

> There is encouragement here. Ultimately, it is God himself who is the guarantor of the gospel. It is his responsibility to preserve it ... We may see the evangelical faith, the faith of the gospel, everywhere spoken against, and the apostolic message of the New Testament ridiculed. We may have to watch an increasing apostasy in the church, as our generation abandons the faith of its fathers. Do not be afraid! God will never allow the light of the gospel to be finally extinguished.[1]

What an encouragement, what a relief. As Barrett says, 'On no other ground would the work of preaching be for a moment endurable.'[2]

Phew! It's not all down to us. And yet ... and yet we are given responsibility. We are given this command. We are to guard the gospel. This most precious possession is not to be treated like a valuable piece of jewellery—taken out only on rare special occasions and the rest of the time hidden away for fear of losing it. That is precisely the way to lose it. We guard it by giving it to future church leaders. Training them to give it away to those who will come after them. That's how we guard the gospel and next, we'll see just how crucial that is.

7

TRAIN LEADERS TO EXPECT DESERTION, BUT TO REJOICE IN FAITHFULNESS

> You know that everyone in the province of Asia has deserted me, including Phygelus and Hermogenes.

— 2 TIMOTHY 1:15

There are many painful experiences in gospel ministry—the rubbish, as my friend calls it. When the rubbish comes we might want to sweep it up, put it in the trash can, tidy things up and press on, but that's easier said than done. Some rubbish leaves a nasty odour and a stain that takes some time to remove. Encounters with some of the rubbish hurts for a long time afterwards. Never is that more the case than when leaders we've partnered with in gospel ministry refuse to stand with us any more. That is extremely painful. That kind of rubbish leaves a bitter taste in the mouth. Or to stretch the 'rubbish' analogy, it leaves a stench up your nostrils and the smell seems to linger for a very long time.

Paul had experienced that kind of rubbish. Sadly, he knew

from bitter experience that being deserted by others was part and parcel of gospel ministry, so he ensured Timothy was ready for it too: 'You know that everyone in the province of Asia has deserted me, including Phygelus and Hermogenes' (2 Timothy 1:15).

This is an astonishing claim. I've no reason to think that this is hyperbole or extreme exaggeration. So listen to it again. Everyone in Asia who had previously worked with Paul in gospel ministry, deserted him, everyone. We don't know how many individuals that 'everyone' amounted to, but we do know the names of two of those who had deserted Paul: Phygelus and Hermogenes. And their desertion was quite unexpected. See how Paul says, *including* Phygelus and Hermogenes? We might say *even* Phygelus and Hermogenes. It seems that they were the last two that Paul would have expected to desert him, and that hurt.

Now let's take a step back and note two things here. First, this comes as an example of people who are ashamed of the gospel. Phygelus and Hermogenes are examples of people who were not prepared to suffer for the gospel. As they are held up as deserters it reinforces precisely why we need to train future gospel leaders, so they know what the gospel is and can expect to suffer for it. It seems the Asian deserters weren't prepared to identify with Paul in prison. They didn't want to be part of a gospel that involved suffering. They deviated from the gospel when it was costly.

Second, we must understand that to desert Paul is to desert the gospel. Back in verse 8 Paul urged Timothy not to 'be ashamed of the testimony about our Lord or of me his prisoner.' To be ashamed of Paul and the gospel he preached and suffered for, is to be ashamed of the gospel of Jesus Christ. Or to put it more starkly, to be ashamed of the gospel that Paul preached and stood for, is to be ashamed of Jesus. Paul was Jesus' apostle (2 Timothy 1:1). Paul was an appointed herald of the gospel. Reject Paul and we reject Jesus.

So Phygelus and Hermogenes desertion of Paul was not just a personal affront against Paul. This was much much more than a couple of Christian men falling out with a Christian leader. In deserting Paul, they were deserting Jesus. Desperately, that happens in gospel ministry. Sometimes the most unexpected people desert the gospel, and Christian leaders need to know that's going to happen, because when it does, it hurts. It's rubbish.

But for all the rubbish, there are wonderful reasons to rejoice. For every trashy experience there are people that are treasures who bring a beautiful aroma into our lives. They are a breath of fresh air when we've been in the rubbish dump. Onesiphorus was one of those people:

> May the Lord show mercy to the household of Onesiphorus, because he often refreshed me and was not ashamed of my chains. On the contrary, when he was in Rome, he searched hard for me until he found me. May the Lord grant that he will find mercy from the Lord on that day! You know very well in how many ways he helped me in Ephesus.
>
> — 2 TIMOTHY 1:16-18

Onesiphorus was the antithesis of Phygelus and Hermogenes. Onesiphorus was the antidote to desertion. He refreshed when others destroyed. Onesiphorus was not ashamed of Paul. He went out of his way, and to great lengths, to find Paul in Rome. Onesiphorus wanted to associate and identify himself with the apostle. He was not ashamed of the gospel, or Paul's chains. He would not flinch from the gospel that had resulted in Paul being imprisoned. Onesiphorus was prepared to stand with Paul even if it meant suffering.

Once again, see how Paul trains Timothy. He tells Timothy what genuine gospel ministry will be like. It will include the deep sadness of people deserting the gospel. But that's not the whole story. There's another side to the coin. For every painful episode of desertion, there's the great joy of those who will go to great lengths to stand with us in proclaiming the great gospel of Jesus Christ. There is a special delight in being in gospel partnership with people who will go out of their way to identify themselves as a gospel person. People who will stand with you, as you stand for Jesus. They refresh you, when you're discouraged.

We must be honest with future Christian leaders about the hardships of gospel ministry. But in the same sentence we must also tell them about the joys. The delights of the Onesiphoruses of this world. They are a sweet perfume that aerate and ventilate. They help us to breath when we feel suffocated by the rubbish.

8

TRAIN LEADERS ON THE JOB

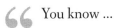 You know ...

— 2 TIMOTHY 1:15

'Know wot I meeen?' was a catchphrase of Ray's. Ray is a great bloke. Salt of the earth. Second generation Brit descended from a Caribbean family, raised in London's East End, 'Know wot I meeen?' It had become an involuntary addition to end every sentence that tumbled out of Ray's 'pie hole' (his expression, not mine—'know wot I meeen?'). Whenever he said it, which was very often, he didn't expect a response! For Ray, 'Know what I meeen?' had become almost worthless, repeated so often, you soon knew not to respond to it. Get to know Ray and in time you'd barely notice his meaningless mantra. 'Know wot I meeen?'

The apostle Paul on the other hand was no Eastender carelessly trotting out redundant catchphrases. So when Paul repeats a phrase we'd do well to take note of it, and think about it. Here in his second letter to Timothy, Paul frequently writes, 'You know.' It comes in 2 Timothy 1:15, 1:18; 2:23; 3:10; 3:14.

The big point is this: because Timothy had lived alongside Paul in ministry, Paul could say to Timothy, 'you know.' 'You know that everyone deserted me' (1:15); 'You know very well in how many ways Onesiphorus helped me in Ephesus' (1:18); 'You, however, know all about my teaching, my way of life, my purpose, faith, patience, love, endurance' (3:10). Paul can say 'you know' because Timothy did know. Paul had shared his life with Timothy. Timothy had served in gospel ministry with Paul. Timothy had seen Paul suffer. Timothy had seen Paul encounter and deal with false teachers and disloyalty. Timothy had seen how Paul responded to disappointment. Paul trained Timothy by sharing his life and ministry with him. Paul trained Timothy on the job and so Timothy had experienced gospel ministry at first-hand, and that is invaluable.

Take the situation we were considering in the last chapter. Paul needed to train Timothy about the pain of desertion and the joy of faithful gospel partnership. He could have simply written, 'Timothy, expect people to desert the faith, even people who have previously been with you in gospel partnership.' That would have taught Timothy what he needed to know, but there's something about experiencing things that can't be replicated in any training manual. First-hand experience puts flesh on the bones in a way that brings the point home with a force and bite that is never forgotten.

In pointing to Phygelus and Hermogenes, Timothy knows that desertion is not a theoretical possibility. More than that, Timothy knows exactly what gospel deserters look like. They can even be normal people like Phygelus and Hermogenes, the sort of people you'd never expect to be turncoats.

You can sit someone down in a classroom and teach them

about the disappointments of gospel ministry but they won't fully grasp how painful it is until they experience it. That's why training gospel leaders can't only be done in a theological college (even though I am very positive about residential theological training).

In his little book *With Him*, Ken Smith advocates always having someone alongside us learning from us the ins and outs, the ups and downs of gospel ministry. He writes:

> I have never heard of a course in seminary entitled, "Persecution." There's a good reason for this: it can't be taught in a classroom! .... Yet by adopting a "with him" approach to discipleship, this will expose learners to their mentor's life and ministry. As men who are being discipled witness such pressure firsthand, this helps to mature them to be ready themselves for the battle.[1]

Richard Bewes testifies to having learned much from his training Vicar, Herbert Cragg. Richard writes:

> Isn't that roughly how it worked with Jesus and His disciples? Most days they were walking together .... following ... eating ... listening and watching. Thus, in any team's development, while 'training seminars' with outside visiting speakers can occupy a useful place, what chiefly matters is *the internal exercise* of standards and attitudes rubbing off from one to another. We work, pray and study together ... forever watching and absorbing along the way. *It's caught as much as taught.*[2]

We see that here in this phrase 'you know.' Because Timothy was alongside Paul in gospel ministry, Timothy knew exactly what Paul was talking about in this letter. He'd seen Paul suffer. He'd seen the way Paul had been deserted. In chapter 2 we discover that Timothy knew people who were false teachers: Hymenaeus and Philetus (2 Timothy 2:17) and it is perhaps in the area of false teaching that this is most critical.

Many people are duped by false teaching because false teachers seem to be so nice. They're pleasant enough. They might even be invested with high office in the church. They speak eloquently. They tell funny stories. They're delightful when you meet them after a service over a cup of tea and a slice of Victoria sponge cake. With their sociable small talk, they're experts at putting you at your ease. All in all they don't appear to be wolves and that's not just because their outfit looks like the clothing of a sheep. So being able to point to 'Harry and Phil' as examples of false teaching, brings it home. False teachers are real flesh and blood people who in every way look very normal. They don't have horns.

Right through this letter Paul illustrates what he means by pointing to characters that 'you know, Timothy.' These characters are often cited in pairs, so I've taken to calling them 'The terrible twos of 2 Timothy.' We met the first 'terrible two' in 2 Timothy 1:15—Phygelus and Hermogenes. I've already referred to the second pair of terrible two's in 2 Timothy 2:17— Hymenaeus and Philetus. In chapter 3 Paul teaches Timothy about the godlessness that will come in the last days as he points to Jannes and Jambres. They were a 'terrible two' who loved themselves, who opposed godly leadership and who wrecked the lives of others. Finally at the end of the letter there are two more characters who have caused such hurt: Demas (2 Timothy 4:10) and Alexander the metal worker (2 Timothy 4:14).

Paul isn't naming and shaming people in an unnecessary vindictive attempt to humiliate them. Paul is helping Timothy to understand what desertion, false teaching and gospel opposition looks like 'in the flesh.'

The big point of all this is the indispensable value of training people on the job. By following Paul around, Timothy knew people and situations. 'You know, Timothy.' We learn best when we experience things first-hand. We never forget when we see living examples of genuine faith, or of suffering, or false teaching, or godless living. That's why we must train people on the job and why Paul didn't just train Timothy in the classroom.

That's why we should train future gospel leaders by doing life with them. Doing ministry with them. Sharing everything with them—our experiences, our family life, our mood swings, our hopes, our fears, our pains, our joys, our disappointments, our encounters with false teachers, everything. 'Know wot I meeen?'

9

TRAIN LEADERS TO TRAIN LEADERS

> ... the things you have heard me say in the presence of many witnesses entrust to reliable people who will also be qualified to teach others.
>
> — 2 TIMOTHY 2:2

I love all sport, so every Olympic year I am in 'heaven.' Then I am taken up into the seventh heaven when the athletics begins. I will never forget that 'Super Saturday' at the London Olympics in 2012. In the space of a few minutes an adoring British crowd witnessed three athletics gold medals in the London Stadium, as Mo Farah, Greg Rutherford, and the darling of British athletics, Jessica Ennis, conquered the world's greatest. Having declared my great love of sport and athletics, you won't be surprised to hear me say how much I love a well-worn illustration of 2 Timothy 2:2. It's the illustration of the relay race and it goes like this: we are to pass the baton of the gospel onto reliable people who will in turn pass on the gospel to other reliable people. It's a great illustration. However, I have one problem with it. The way the illustration is usually used puts the focus on the baton. The baton in the illustration is the gospel, so the illustration goes, we are to pass on the gospel to other people who in turn pass on the gospel and so on.

It's a terrific point which I share wholeheartedly, but it's not quite sharp enough to fully understand the emphasis of 2 Timothy 2:2. What Paul is telling Timothy to do here is greater than passing on the gospel. For sure he is saying that. We saw in chapter 1:9-10 that we must train future leaders in gospel truth. It is crucial and critical that we pass on the authentic gospel. But there's more. The emphasis in 2:2 is that we must pass on the gospel to reliable people. Returning to the illustration of the relay race, the focus here is on the runners themselves (the team) and not just the baton (the gospel). This verse is as much about team selection, as it is about getting the baton round the track. The critical thing for Timothy to know is that he must be someone who identifies and trains reliable people. That's a key development in the letter from chapter 1 to chapter 2. Take the immediate context: 'You then, my son, be strong in the grace that is in Christ Jesus' (2 Timothy 2:1).

Chapter 1 has ended with a stark contrast. The contrast between those who desert Paul, and therefore desert the gospel (typified by Phygelus and Hermogenes) and those who remain faithful to Paul, namely Onesiphorus. So, says Paul to Timothy, 'make sure you are on the side of the angels.' 'Be like Onesiphorus.' 'Be strong in the grace that is in Christ Jesus' (2 Timothy 2:1). This is not just 'be strong' but 'be strong in grace.' Timothy, be strong in the grace of the gospel. And then, as a leader who is strong in the gospel, be sure to find others to train: 'the things you have heard me say in the presence of many witnesses entrust to reliable people who will also be qualified to teach others' (2 Timothy 2:2).

This verse adduces four generations of gospel leaders. First Paul taught Timothy (that's two generations), then Timothy is to find and pass on the gospel to reliable people (three), then the reliable people that Timothy trains are to pass on the gospel to reliable people (four). Of course, this 'training leaders, who train leaders to train leaders' is not to stop after four generations. Paul is setting a pattern of gospel leaders training gospel leaders. He is demonstrating how training the next generation is an essential part of faithful gospel ministry.

So how do we train people to train people? That's what this book is about. Here, simply see that it's a stated task, a priority if you will. And in the context of desertion, we see why it's so critical and why the emphasis is on looking for *reliable* people. Faithful people. We've seen in Phygelus and Hermogenes what a disaster it is when Christian leaders are unreliable and unfaithful. Timothy needs to look to train people like Onesiphorus, people who are reliable, people who know, hold onto, and then pass on the gospel. Reliable people are those prepared to suffer for the gospel. Reliable people are those who won't be ashamed of the gospel even when it will cost them. And it will cost them.

As we saw in chapter one of this book, the need to train the next generation of Christian leaders is central to 2 Timothy. Facing death, Paul knew he had done that work. See here how he had not just trained Timothy and so left the church in good hands for one more generation, but that he trained Timothy to train others to train others. Training the next generation of faithful leaders to be trainers of the next generation is part of what it means to exercise faithful gospel ministry. In having the gospel, we have the baton, now we must ensure that we not only pass it on, but that we pass it on to people who will pass it on to the right people. That's how to run the race and win the world.

TRAIN LEADERS TO BE SACRIFICIAL AND HARDWORKING

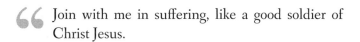

66 Join with me in suffering, like a good soldier of
Christ Jesus.

— 2 TIMOTHY 2:3

A former colleague of mine was given considerable responsibility and influence in the Church of England. He used it brilliantly for the gospel. One of the key ways he used his position was to fashion openings for good gospel men into positions of church leadership. But speaking at a national conference he gently shared one great frustration. On too many occasions, having negotiated openings for gospel men to lead churches, they would then turn down the opportunity because of the house! The man, or his wife, or both, would express their dissatisfaction with the property that the church would provide for them. The kitchen was too small. They were hoping for a guest bedroom in which their in-laws could stay when they visited. The house isn't in a fashionable neighbourhood. I was shocked when I heard him say these things. People are being paid to tell people about Jesus, and being provided with living accommodation, and they're sniffy about the house. It was some years ago that I heard my friend express his concern and since hearing him, I've encountered it myself. People in gospel ministry, in the leafy suburbs of England, complain about all manner of aspects of their living conditions.

A couple of years ago the mission committee of the church I'm part of, asked me to visit our mission partners working with people in the slum community in Phnom Penh, Cambodia. It was a life-changing experience. I will never forget some of the sights I saw. I will show restraint and resist the temptation to express my creative writing skills at this point. I don't want to be accused of being gratuitous. But you'll understand that some of the sights from that trip left a profound impression on me. For now, it's enough to tell you that the conditions people live in in the slums are utterly degrading. Day after day, Jonathan and Zoe (the mission partners I visited), walked into the slum community and shared the good news of Jesus with these dear poverty-stricken people. As they did, Jonathan and Zoe opened themselves to disease and all sorts of dangers. Meanwhile, here we are living in England's green and pleasant land, enjoying all the benefits of an endless stream of clean running water, central heating, locks on the doors, safe sewage, electricity, food in the cupboards, a whole wardrobe of clothes to wear (I don't need to embellish my list further—we all know how comfortable it is for us living in 21st-century Britain). So it rather grates to hear people complain that the kitchen isn't big enough and they'd rather hoped for a guest bedroom.

I have now taken to telling gospel ministers that they need to consider themselves to be missionaries (because that's what they are). They need to live a life of sacrificial service. Nineteenth-century missionaries left their homes with all their worldly possessions packed in a coffin, because they expected to die on the mission field and never return to their homeland. Yet, here in Britain in the 21st century, people who chose to be in Christian leadership can't 'squeeze' into a three bedroomed house. Try reading Paul's words and see how the desire for comfort and ease squares with the type of leaders we should train up:

> Join with me in suffering, like a good soldier of Christ Jesus. No one serving as a soldier gets entangled in civilian affairs, but rather tries to please his commanding officer. Similarly, anyone who competes as an athlete does not receive the victor's crown except by competing according to the rules. The hardworking farmer should be the first to receive a share of the crops.
>
> — 2 TIMOTHY 2:3-6

We must select future Christian leaders who are prepared for a hard life. Gospel ministry is a life of sacrifice and hardship. In order to help us see the nature of gospel ministry Paul selects three powerful images: the soldier, the athlete and the farmer. Tellingly, all three 'professions' involve sacrifice and hard work. Much could be said from each picture. We'd do well to stop and reflect on each of them and ask the Lord to give us insight into their bearing on gospel ministry because that is precisely what Paul tells Timothy to do in verse 7: 'Reflect on what I am saying, for the Lord will give you insight into all this' (2 Timothy 2:7).

It won't take much reflection to conclude that there are some things that are true of all three pictures. Life in the military, training to be an athlete, and farming, all involve dedicated hard work. All three involve sacrifice. A soldier sacrifices his freedoms. He follows orders and goes wherever he's deployed. He doesn't chose where to live or what his house will look like (which is interesting following our earlier considerations).

Athletes have to be incredibly disciplined in their training. Their routine includes pushing through the pain barrier, watching what they eat, and getting to bed on time. A victorious few athletes enjoy brief moments of success, but whether they are winners or 'also rans,' every athlete spends thousands of hours a year following an unglamorous and exhausting training regime.

Farmers never enjoy the victorious accolades of the successful athlete or the triumphant solider. They work incredibly hard all year round. There's never much social life or free time on the farm. Then at harvest time, or lambing season it gets ramped up a few extra notches. Week after tiring week, up at the crack of dawn, and to bed only when the sun goes down.

It seems to me that Paul has quite deliberately chosen these three professions as illustrations of gospel ministry so that we know that church leadership involves hard work and sacrifice. But he also specifies one further application from each picture.

1. THE SOLDIER (VERSES 3-4): NOT GETTING INVOLVED IN CIVILIAN AFFAIRS

As we've already considered Paul states that gospel ministry is one of hardship, like being in the military (verse 3). We should expect it to be tough. But the specific thing he highlights about soldiers is that they don't get involved in civilian affairs because they want to please their commander.

There are all sorts of 'civilian affairs' we can be distracted by. I live in one of the most beautiful parts of Britain. We are surrounded by beautiful hills and delightful homes. I love playing tennis and my house overlooks the last grass tennis courts in Sheffield. You won't be surprised to know we have a television in our house. Hill walking, tennis playing and television watching can be huge distractions for me (you'll have your own). Now please don't mishear me: those things aren't wrong (or they needn't be). Paul told Timothy in his first letter that 'everything God created is good, and nothing is to be rejected if it is received with thanksgiving' (1 Timothy 4:4). So the hills are good. Walking in the Peak District is good. It is easy to praise God and to be thankful while enjoying the spectacular views at the top of Kinder Scout or scrabbling up a rocky crag onto Curbar Edge. There's nothing wrong with appreciating God's creation. But I must be sure that I'm not distracted by civilian affairs. My task as a minister of the gospel is to be focussed on the campaign to take the gospel to a lost world. That means sacrifice. Not spending hours watching sport on the television or playing tennis or even hill walking. My focus and delight needs to be in pleasing my commanding officer.

2. THE ATHLETE (VERSE 5): COMPETING ACCORDING TO THE RULES

We've already considered how disciplined and focussed athletes must be. That is a significant part of the point of the picture of the athlete (note the word 'similarly'—just like soldiers). But Paul further emphasises one thing about the athlete: they must compete according to the rules. Anyone who's watched any athletics knows the truth of this. The 100 metre sprinter who sets off before the gun is fired is disqualified.

The 200 metre runner who strays into another athlete's lane while taking the bend is disqualified. The cheat who takes a banned substance to enhance their performance is disqualified when their blood sample is positive. The picture is obvious. But what does it mean for Christian leadership? Well, it cannot be about the need to live up to a moral code. We believe in a gospel of grace. Grace ensures we'll receive the prize despite our numerous and gargantuan moral failures. No, the need to compete according to the rules is about the importance of the leader not departing from the gospel. That's been the context all along. Christian leaders must unflinchingly hold on to the revealed gospel of grace and be ready to stand for it, even when it results in suffering. If you break that rule, as Phygelus and Hermogenes did, then you won't receive the victor's crown. Because to depart from the apostolic gospel is to separate yourself from Jesus.

3. THE FARMER (VERSE 6): THE FIRST TO RECEIVE A SHARE OF THE CROPS

Again, we've considered how tough it is being a farmer. And Paul wants us to see that, as he introduces the *hardworking* farmer. But again there's one specific thing he mentions, the share of the crop, which the farmer is first to receive. Paul is of course pointing to the wonderful harvest at the end of the age that we'll enjoy. Yes, gospel ministry is tough. It involves hard graft and making sacrifices, but that's not all there is to say. The final 'reward' on that final day will make all the struggles more than worthwhile.

In all three pictures then there is both a challenge and a wonderful encouragement.

Gospel workers are to be ready for hard work and sacrifice.

Specifically avoiding distraction (the soldier), sticking to the rules of proclaiming the gospel (the athlete) and working hard (the farmer). And our motivation is the wonderful encouragement of pleasing our commanding officer (the soldier), receiving the victor's crown (the athlete) and being the first to receive a share of the crop (the farmer).

We must teach gospel workers that gospel ministry is hard work and that it involves sacrifice, but in the same breath, we can spell out the wonderful benefits and motivations to keep going. That way Christian leaders should be ready for the fight, and strenuous training, and hard graft, and be able to avoid the temptation to crave a bigger kitchen and a guest bedroom. We do after all have something much greater to look forward to: a room in a wonderful heavenly mansion!

11

TRAIN LEADERS TO FOCUS ON CHRIST WHO SUFFERED AND WAS GLORIFIED

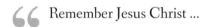 Remember Jesus Christ ...

— 2 TIMOTHY 2:8

Ever since the appalling carnage of 9/11 the 21st century has been blighted by a rise in global terrorism. Not many weeks go by without news headlines being dominated by another attack on innocent civilians somewhere, in the name of a terrorist organisation. In the corridors of power, the greatest military strategists are using the most sophisticated intelligence in an attempt to at least thwart terrorist activity, even if they cannot eradicate it. Only time will tell how historians will reflect on this menace of our time. But whatever the historians make of it all, one thing about current global terrorism that needs to be pointed out is that its overlords are cowards. They persuade young, impressionable people to strap explosives to themselves, while they themselves bunker down in a hide-out in the hills. Contrast the cowardly leaders of terrorist organisations with Jesus Christ. He doesn't ask any of his followers to do anything that he hasn't already done himself.

From 2 Timothy 1:8 onwards, Paul has expressed the need to tell Christian leaders that they will suffer for the gospel. In the last chapter we saw that when training future leaders we must impress upon them that gospel leadership is hard work and sacrificial. Paul led by example in this, being chained for the gospel (2 Timothy 1:16). But while Paul is an example to follow, there's one who is the example par excellence. Paul writes, 'Remember Jesus Christ' (2 Timothy 2:8).

In this section Paul urges Timothy (and all Christian leaders) to look to Jesus for our motivation and pattern of Christian leadership. The big thing Paul emphasises in this section is that the way of Christian leadership, modelled by the Lord himself, is suffering followed by glory.

Before we consider that in detail, don't miss the simple but profound wisdom of remembering Jesus Christ. Regularly fixing our gaze on him will motivate us and inspire us and urge us on our way, not least when it's tough. We saw in 2 Timothy 1:12 that the gospel is about a person, not just about a body of belief. Paul states it unequivocally here, 'Remember Jesus Christ, raised from the dead, descended from David. This is my gospel' (verse 8). Jesus is the subject of the gospel. We must be sure to train Christian leaders to remember Jesus Christ. To look to him daily. To reflect on him daily. To remember his life daily. There's no substitute for looking at our substitute.

For me, remembering Jesus means spending much time in the gospels. Please don't misunderstand me. I believe the whole Bible is the inspired Word of God. I don't believe that the gospels or the words of the Lord recorded in the gospels are more inspired than the rest of Scripture. I also believe the whole Bible points to Jesus (John 5:39). But, with all these caveats clearly stated, I do find it hugely beneficial in my own daily devotions, to go back again and again to the gospels. There, in the gospels, I see Jesus most clearly. It is remembering Jesus Christ that will keep me going and motivate me to suffer for him because he first suffered for me.

So remember Jesus Christ. But what is it we are specifically to remember about him?

> Remember Jesus Christ, raised from the dead, descended from David. This is my gospel, for which I am suffering even to the point of being chained like a criminal. But God's word is not chained. Therefore I endure everything for the sake of the elect, that they too may obtain the salvation that is in Christ Jesus, with eternal glory
>
> — 2 TIMOTHY 2:8-10

In the first half of chapter 2 we saw that the way of Christian leadership is tough. It's really hard work. It involves sacrifice. It's the life of the soldier, the athlete and the farmer all rolled into one. Yes, there are glorious 'benefits' but they are largely future rewards. The way of Christian leadership is suffering now and glory later. That's one thing we're to see as we remember Jesus Christ, because that is precisely the pattern of life he followed.

Jesus Christ was raised from the dead (verse 8). He died first and then he was raised to life. Suffering death first and then raised to glory.

Jesus was descended from David (Verse 8). David was the king who suffered under Saul before he experienced the glory of being made Israel's King. Suffering first, followed by glory later.

This is the gospel for which Paul is suffering even to the point of being chained up like a dog, as a criminal (verse 9).

Paul was prepared to suffer for the gospel because he remembered Jesus Christ. His Lord suffered first and then glory followed. So Paul will suffer because he knows that glory will follow. Tellingly, the glory that Paul looks forward to is the eternal glory to be enjoyed by those who hear his gospel message. He is motivated by glory to come, but he still had to suffer first:

> Therefore I endure everything for the sake of the elect, that they too may obtain the salvation that is in Christ Jesus, with eternal glory
>
> — 2 TIMOTHY 2:10

Paul knew that he could be chained up, but the Word of the gospel that he preached could not be chained. The Word is dynamic and would work to save people and bring them to glory (verse 10).

The big point is this, we must remember Jesus Christ, because in him we see the pattern of the Christian life, and specifically the pattern of Christian leadership: first suffering, and only then, glory to follow.

Right through this section we're presented with this same pattern. Suffering is part of the Christian gospel, but it will be followed by glory. It's a pattern that tells us it's worth suffering for the gospel as this trustworthy saying endorses,

> If we died with him, we will also live with him; if

we endure, we will also reign with him. If we disown him, he will also disown us; if we are faithless, he remains faithful, for he cannot disown himself.

— 2 TIMOTHY 2:11-13

Verses 11 and 12a emphasise the very fact of suffering now and glory later. 'If we died with him, we will also live with him; if we endure we will also reign with him' (verses 11-12a). So keep going. Be ready to die with Christ. Endure to the end. Don't be like Phygelus and Hermogenes who didn't keep going. Because if we endure through suffering, we will one day reign with Jesus. Keep going, Timothy; don't timidly shrink under pressure. Look ahead: glory awaits. Reigning with Christ is the glorious reward to come. But we must keep going because:

66 If we disown him, he will also disown us; if we are faithless, he remains faithful, for he cannot disown himself.

— 2 TIMOTHY 2:12-13

This trustworthy saying teaches the next generation of gospel leaders that it's worth suffering now because glory will follow. But it also warns leaders of the dangers of disowning the Lord, the way Phygelus and Hermogenes did, because if we disown the Lord, we will be disowned by him. God is faithful to his word of judgement. He must be faithful to himself, so he will disown faithless people.

Christian leadership is tough. So look to *the* leader. See how different he is from other leaders all over the world and not least, all the leaders of global terrorism. He doesn't ask us to do anything he hasn't already been through. Indeed, what he suffered is far worse than anything we'll ever be expected to endure. So, remember Jesus Christ. Have your eyes fixed on him. See how he set the pattern for Christian life and leadership—he suffered for the lost, and was crowned in glory. Suffer for the gospel knowing that one day we will live and reign with him in glory.

12

TRAIN LEADERS TO BE CAREFUL WITH WORDS

> Warn them before God against quarreling about words; it is of no value, and only ruins those who listen.

> — 2 TIMOTHY 2:14

'Sticks and stones may break my bones but words will never hurt me.' It's the great playground repost. The school playground can be one of the cruellest places on the planet. Spiteful seven year old kids have a go at the new, shy six year old, sometimes physically, often verbally. The school playground is like a war zone, which is why dinner ladies have to be experts in conflict management!

So when children are verbally abused, we teach them that little ditty. We teach them to tell the name callers, 'a physical beating might leave a scar, but nothing you can say will leave its mark.' It sounds good, but the problem is, it's not true. Indeed, barring the most horrific physical injuries, it's far more likely that a recurrent vindictive verbal lashing will cause the more significant and terrible scars of mental anguish and long-term psychological injury. I have met many people who are seriously emotionally damaged by the things that were repeatedly said to them when they were growing up. Words are powerful. But then all Christians know that; we are people of the Word. The Word transforms. It was the Word that brought everything into being in the first place. The Word changes lives. God's Word cannot be chained (2 Timothy 2:9). Words are powerful. So we must be sure that we teach Christian leaders to be very careful with words:

 Keep reminding God's people of these things. Warn them before God against quarreling about words; it is of no value, and only ruins those who listen. Do your best to present yourself to God as one approved, a worker who does not need to be ashamed and who correctly handles the word of truth.

— 2 TIMOTHY 2:14-15

Here, Paul is teaching Timothy what he should teach: 'Keep reminding them' (verse 14), 'them' being the reliable future Christian leaders of verse 2 of this chapter. Timothy is to keep reminding them that it is possible to be disqualified and thrown off track and not receive the victor's crown. So Timothy, keep reminding future gospel leaders how it's quite possible to depart from the gospel. And keep reminding them that false teaching is one of the dangers that throws us off track. So in this section, Paul teaches Timothy how to stand against false teaching and false teachers. But before he gets right into the problem of false teaching, he addresses something that seems quite innocuous: 'Don't quarrel about words' he says. Except that isn't all that he says. A careful reading makes it clear that Paul thinks this is far from harmless. He writes: 'Warn them before God against quarreling about words' (2 Timothy 2:14).

'Warn them before God' shows the seriousness of what is being said. It seems that quarrelling about words is more important than we might think. Quarrelling about words can be toxic.

Let's be clear here: this can't be a prohibition against calling out false teaching. Error must be confronted and addressed. I reckon this could be addressing one of two things:

First, young men love an argument. Pride means we want to prove ourselves right. Remember Paul is teaching Timothy how to train the next cohort of gospel leaders. This quarrelling could be about insignificant words. It takes me back to my days at theological college. Largely, I loved my time training for gospel ministry. But there were times when we used to enter into verbal spats about all sorts of things that really weren't that important. I seem to remember voices being raised in the common room about the materials used to build the Tower of Babel! Don't mishear me. Precise theology is very important (we'll see that in a few verses time). In many ways we should be pedants—words matter. But we mustn't get picky over things that don't matter. That's more often about pride, and winning an argument, and when people hear leaders arguing about insignificant things, it ruins them.

Second, this command might have an eye on the false teachers, which is the big thrust of the rest of this section. Paul has already pointed out to Timothy how quarrelling about words is a key characteristic of false teachers (1 Timothy 6:3-5). So this might be a reminder that getting involved in debates with false teachers is not helpful. It doesn't build people up, it tears them down; it's destructive.

Whichever of the two this is referring to, the point is clear. Arguments about words ruins those who hear it (2 Timothy 2:14). On the other hand: 'Do your best to present yourself to God as one approved, a worker who does not need to be ashamed and who correctly handles the word of truth' (2 Timothy 2:15).

Timothy is to be an example to those he trains. He will do that by correctly handling the Word of God rather than arguing about words; those who correctly handle the Word of truth are approved workers of God.

I know nothing about cars, so, for me, buying a new one is a precarious business. Any unscrupulous mechanic or used car salesman could bamboozle me with talk about the need to regularly service the overhead underhang on the manifold crankshaft. Talk technicalities about cars and you could take me in hook, line and sinker. So I'm thrilled that reputable global motor companies have taken much of the lottery out of the second-hand car market by approving Used Cars. The company will have their engineers look over second-hand cars, ensure they are sound and sell them with a warranty, as cars approved by the maker. It's not a perfect illustration, but when leaders correctly handle the Word of God, they have 'approved by God' stamped on them.

Christian leaders have a responsibility when it comes to words. We can be those who quarrel about small and insignificant theological details, or we can put all our energy into being teachers who correctly handle the Word of God. If we get caught up in the first we'll ruin those who hear us. If we do the latter, we'll show ourselves to be God's approved workers.

Training the next generation of gospel workers includes reminding them of the importance and power of words and impressing on them the need to handle the Word of truth correctly. Contrary to the little playground ditty, words can really hurt.

13

TRAIN LEADERS TO WORK HARD IN THE WORD

> Do your best to present yourself to God as one approved, a worker who does not need to be ashamed and who correctly handles the word of truth.

— 2 TIMOTHY 2:15

Teaching the Bible is hard work. I'm not thinking about the actual task of preaching, leading a Bible study or meeting someone for a one to one. All those activities can be hard work. It's not unusual for preachers to feel exhausted and even depressed after preaching a sermon. Leading small group Bible studies can, at times, feel like herding cats! Studying the Bible with an individual can be frustrating when they seem to take one step forward and two back. That said, when we see people understanding and growing in the faith, teaching the Bible can be the most thrilling and invigorating experience.

When I say that Bible teaching is hard work I'm thinking primarily about the work that no-one sees, the work in the study. By the end of a morning's work I often feel worn out. Which is strange because it's not as if I'm like the man digging a hole in the road, who has arms like tree trunks and whose labours cause sweat to run down his back. A morning in the study consists of nothing physical at all. I sit at my desk reading and thinking about the Bible. What's exhausting about that? I hardly move a muscle, except mid-morning when I exert myself to make a cup of tea or to retrieve a commentary from the bookshelf. What's so tiring about that?

In this verse Paul describes the person who handles the Word of truth as a worker. It's the same idea as the hardworking farmer, athlete, soldier. We completely understand why those serving in the military, or engaging in athletics training, or working in agriculture, fall into bed exhausted at the end of the day. But surprisingly, handling the Word of truth is hard work too. There's a mental and spiritual 'strain' that is exacting and demanding. We don't have to move a muscle to study the Bible, but we have to muster all the energy we have to engage the 'muscles' of heart and mind. Anyone who's ever put their mind to the task will know what I'm talking about and what hard work it is.

The idea behind 'correctly handling' the Bible, is to 'cut straight.' It's a precise task, with no wonky 'cutting' allowed. Lee Gatiss writes, 'an orthodox teacher will give right glory to God by giving God's word to people straight, neither reading into it what is not there, nor leaving out something which people need to hear, nor twisting it to suit their own purposes.'[1]

Anyone can look at the Bible and say something about it or from it. Sit in small group Bible studies and listen to the ideas people come up with off the top of their head and without much thought. It's easy to say something about a passage of the Bible. But to make a true cut through the Word and not deliver a deviating wander through the Scriptures requires careful accuracy. To be a faithful Bible teacher, correctly handling the Word of truth, is a precision task and it involves concentrated hard work.

When we're handling the Bible in order to teach it, we are dealing with the very words of life—they can bring eternal life. We could hardly be participating in anything more important. There's a weight of responsibility in Bible teaching. It's vital that we get it right. We dare not get it wrong. The pressure is on; that's why it's such hard work.

Paul is encouraging Timothy here to be a workman who has no need to be ashamed of his Bible handling, but to be one who correctly handles the Word of truth. It is incumbent upon us to train people in the task of Bible handling. To do that, we must model it, when training others. That's the immediate context. Timothy is to keep reminding and warning future leaders about the power of words. One key way he'll do that is by ensuring that he correctly handles God's Word.

In the demands of regular gospel ministry it's easy to slip into the habit of churning out talks, or to settle for shoddy workmanship in order to get a talk written. But we need to be those who always correctly handle the Word of truth, especially when we're training others. They'll be watching our every move, listening to our every word. That's hard work.

It's precisely because it is such hard work, that the Bible teacher will be tempted to be lazy and to cut corners rather than cut straight. In some ways the temptation to slack off in the study becomes greater as we get older and become more adept at saying something true, without precisely teaching what a passage teaches.

From day one, we need to train leaders that Bible teaching is hard work, and that it will always be hard work. As the

Australian evangelist, John Chapman used to say of Bible teaching, 'The first 60 years are the hardest.' We need to walk into the study each morning as if we were labourers digging holes, knowing we're in for a strenuous morning. The hole won't be dug without hard graft. Similarly, cutting straight and true through a Bible passage won't happen without tough, sustained, hard work. When training gospel workers it's imperative that we show them what good Bible teaching looks like by handling the Bible correctly ourselves. And they need to understand that Bible handling is no walk in the park. It demands that we give everything we can. It's enough to leave anyone exhausted at the end of the day.

14

TRAIN LEADERS TO AVOID PLAYING
AROUND WITH DODGY THEOLOGY

 Avoid godless chatter, because those who indulge
in it will become more and more ungodly.

— 2 TIMOTHY 2:16

At theological college I remember a discussion in the
common room concerning how many angels could dance
on the point of a pin. Never mind the point of a pin, there was
no point to the discussion! In some ways it was a harmless
exchange of views in an environment where we were rightly
encouraged to think for ourselves and reflect theologically.
However the fact that so many people pitched in with an
opinion is an indication of one of the great temptations for
church leaders, namely to get unhelpfully caught up in fanciful
ideas. The peril of such involvement is twofold: first, it has the
potential to spread dangerous teaching. Second, it can harm
those who get involved in it.

Having been warned not to quarrel about words, but rather
to handle the Word of God correctly, in 2 Timothy 2:16-18

Paul gives concrete examples of how to work this out. Positively, we can avoid the harmful effects of false teaching by not getting involved with it ourselves. Paul writes, 'Avoid godless chatter, because those who indulge in it will become more and more ungodly' (2 Timothy 2:16).

'Godless chatter' here is not the temptation to talk about the latest plot line in *Eastenders* or to join in the office gossip. 'Godless chatter' here means an unhealthy interest in false teaching. Faithful leaders are to avoid the temptation to be drawn into fanciful theological ideas. Again, this is not telling us to refrain from engaging with false teaching; it's not a suggestion that we should never interact with new or novel theological concepts, although a previous boss of mine helpfully warned me away from anything 'new.' His point? If it's not been embraced by the church in the last 2,000 years of Christian history, it's unlikely to be helpful today.

That said, it's obvious that Christian leaders must engage with, and think about theology at every level. But there's a difference between 'engaging with' and 'indulging in' (that's the word in verse 16). Indulging in false teaching (godless chatter) is to allow myself to begin to 'play around with' novel theological ideas. To try it on for size. Maybe to 'fly a theological kite' with the congregation. Or perhaps test something out in a small group. That, I think, is the godless chatter Paul is warning Timothy about here. When we begin to spread unconventional (or maybe I should say, unorthodox) teaching, it has two harmful effects.

First, we'll become 'more and more ungodly' (verse 16). Teaching false ideas is self-harming. That's because godliness is inextricably tied to theology. Truth shapes us; we are to be transformed by the renewing of our minds (Romans 12:2). What we believe and what we teach is what we become. To teach anything we have to in some measure adopt it. Once we begin to teach unorthodox ideas, we will become unorthodox in the way we live and so 'godless chatter' will prove harmful to us.

Second, godless chatter has a devastating effect on others. The moment we teach 'ideas' that are not pure, we are spreading something that is unhealthy and very harmful to others. That's what false teachers are doing. 'Their teaching will spread like gangrene' (2 Timothy 2:17).

Gangrene is very dangerous. If it's not stopped, it kills. Gangrenous limbs often have to be amputated in order to save life. False teaching is like gangrene—it has to be cut off in order to save lives. To be involved in godless chatter is to spread the infection and reinforce the impact of false teaching, Paul points Timothy to Hymenaeus and Philetus:

 Their teaching will spread like gangrene. Among them are Hymenaeus and Philetus, who have departed from the truth. They say that the resurrection has already taken place, and they destroy the faith of some.

— 2 TIMOTHY 2:17-18

Hymenaeus and Philetus are the second terrible two of 2 Timothy. Because Timothy has served alongside Paul, he knows exactly who Hymenaeus and Philetus are and he knows precisely the impact their teaching had on others. They had a fanciful notion that the resurrection of the dead had already occurred. The precise nature of their error needn't concern us (let's not get involved in godless chatter!). The important thing to note is the impact their teaching had—it destroyed the faith of some.

Sadly, on more than one occasion, I've seen very able young Bible teachers being influenced by strong personalities teaching slightly wonky theology. It started as a stimulating conversation about an interesting idea discussed over a coffee. Then they began to pass it on to others who found it fascinating and stimulating. Eventually it became a major theological emphasis in their teaching and theological framework. In the process they began to teach it to others and sadly it destroyed the faith of some. We must train young potential church leaders to avoid godless chatter: we must impress upon them the dangers of playing around with dodgy theology.

15

TRAIN LEADERS TO BELIEVE IN THE DOCTRINE OF GOD'S ELECT

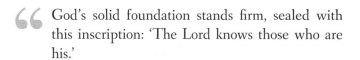 God's solid foundation stands firm, sealed with this inscription: 'The Lord knows those who are his.'

— 2 TIMOTHY 2:19

Really caring for others can leave you overwhelmed with worry: just ask the parents of teenagers! Church leaders should care for their church family. But when they do, hearing what Timothy has just read could leave the church leader beside themselves with worry. False teaching destroys the faith of some. False teaching will rob people of the eternal prize. With the stakes so high, you might expect Paul to urge Timothy to be on the lookout for false teaching and to wage an all-out-war on anyone like Hymenaeus and Philetus. But no—the next thing Paul writes is:

Nevertheless, God's solid foundation stands firm, sealed with this inscription: "The Lord knows those who are his," and, "Everyone who confesses the name of the Lord must turn away from wickedness."

— 2 TIMOTHY 2:19

Knowing that false teaching destroys the faith of some, we need the wonderful reassurance that God's elect will not be lost. 'The Lord knows those who are his.'

Again and again we've seen that when Paul teaches a big truth, very often, the next thing he does is bring a balancing truth immediately onto the page. Yes, we should be concerned about the gangrenous effect of false teaching. Yes, we should be concerned for those under our pastoral care, but not to the point of being out of our minds and worried sick about the salvation of people. We'll be rescued from that anxiety when we are sure that 'the Lord knows who are his and will keep them safe forever.'[1] That's the foundation on which we stand. There's great assurance here.

I love the way this verse balances the previous warning of the impact of false teaching. For years I worked at life in ministry as if everything depended on me. My evangelistic fervour was driven by an underlying sense that if I didn't tell people, they wouldn't be saved. That left me terribly burdened, believing that my faithful teaching was the only way to protect those under my care. It might appear laudable, but it's likely to make you uptight and edgy and it's sure to lead to many a sleepless night, or worse.

To save ourselves from a cardiac arrest we need this inscription, 'The Lord knows those who are his' (2 Timothy

2:19). Believing that the salvation of others is not all down to my evangelistic efforts and knowing that the keeping of God's people is not all down to my ability to counter false teaching will go a long way to rescuing me from burnout. So we must teach the next generation of gospel workers to believe in the doctrine of God's elect. Not just to believe it as a doctrine to assent to intellectually, but to believe it, and live it out, so that it changes the way we conduct ourselves in life and ministry. Of course, that doesn't mean that the doctrine of election is an excuse to be laissez-faire about godly Christian living. Again see the wonderful balance in this verse. There's a second inscription we need to read: 'Everyone who confesses the name of the Lord must turn away from wickedness' (2 Timothy 2:19).

Election is never a reason to play fast and loose with salvation. Indeed, the elect will demonstrate their election in desiring to live a holy life. So, yes, teach truth. Stand against false teaching. Pastor people to stay away from false teaching and tell them how they should live. When you really care for people you'll be concerned for them. But do all that in the assurance that the Lord knows his own and will keep his own. Then you'll be able to sleep at night, even when the wolves are prowling around and teaching erroneous and harmful doctrines. 'The Lord knows who are his.'

16

TRAIN LEADERS TO UNDERSTAND THE GOOD THAT COMES FROM FALSE TEACHING IN THE CHURCH

> In a large house there are articles not only of gold and silver, but also of wood and clay.

— 2 TIMOTHY 2:20

No, you've not misread the title of this chapter, and it's not a typographical error. False teaching does the church good! Don't misunderstand me; false teaching in itself is never good. We should never rejoice in anything that contradicts God, or in any contravention of his Word. Anything that could harm his people is to be abhorred. But that said, false teaching in the church can be used by God to make us the people we ought to be.

Hymenaeus and Philetus, the false teachers cited by Paul in chapter 2, v17 are dangerous. They, and people like them, destroy the faith of some, a very serious matter. But still, having false teachers around has a cleansing effect on the church. That's the next thing Paul teaches Timothy:

> In a large house there are articles not only of gold and silver, but also of wood and clay; some are for special purposes and some for common use. Those who cleanse themselves from the latter will be instruments for special purposes, made holy, useful to the Master and prepared to do any good work.

> — 2 TIMOTHY 2:20-21

Allow me to suggest that the large house in this picture is the visible church (1 Timothy 3:14-15). In any household some items are used for noble purposes and some for dishonourable purposes. Take a salad bowl. It has a noble task—you toss a delicious caesar salad in your salad bowl. It looks great, tastes delicious and is nutritious. Your salad bowl has a noble purpose. On the other hand, take a scrubbing brush. It has a vital role to play in getting rid of the dirt and grime that's been trampled onto the kitchen floor. But unlike your salad bowl, your scrubbing brush is kept out of sight, tucked away in the cleaning cupboard, and you'd certainly never put it on the dining room table. The scrubbing brush has an ignoble purpose in the house.

Hymenaeus and Philetus are in the church. You wouldn't hold them up as people to follow. You certainly wouldn't give them a platform from which to peddle their life-threatening theories of the resurrection. You would never, as it were, put them on the dining room table and give even the slightest suggestion that what comes out of them is nutritious. But, all the same, God is using them and their teaching to clean up the church.

When everything is going well in a church, we can become lazy. Careful Bible reading doesn't seem to be so critical. Being sharp on doctrine doesn't appear to be so necessary. Prayer isn't so urgent or impassioned. It's easy in good times to get a bit theologically flabby. But when false teaching arrives on the scene, it makes everyone sit up. To use the language in Paul's illustration, it cleans up the church. False teaching makes us read our Bibles more carefully, pay more attention to doctrine and it makes us pray more fervently. God uses false teachers like Hymenaeus and Philetus, as a kind of scrubbing brush. False teaching helps to get the church clean:

> Those who cleanse themselves from the [false teachers] will be instruments for special purposes, made holy, useful to the Master and prepared to do any good work.

> — 2 TIMOTHY 2:21

This is such an encouraging thing to teach the next generation of gospel workers. The battle against false teaching is wearing and tiresome, but when we counter it and stand against it, it has a cleansing effect on us, making us more useful to the Lord and preparing us for any good work for him.

Teaching church leaders that God uses false teaching to make the church cleaner and therefore more useful, is a great encouragement for us to get out our scrubbing brushes when false teaching arrives on our doorsteps.

17

TRAIN LEADERS NOT TO BE QUARRELSOME

 ... the Lord's servant must not be quarrelsome but must be kind to everyone, able to teach, not resentful.

— 2 TIMOTHY 2:24

There are some people who seem to enjoy a good argument. I used to be like that. These days, when I meet people that I used to be like, I realise how exhausting and frustrating it must have been to have me around! You can find quarrelsome characters of every age, but young men are especially prone to it. Thinking back to my own predilection to be argumentative, while I would have justified it in my own mind as a desire for accuracy and truth, in reality, it was largely born of pride. I wanted to show that I was right. I wanted people to believe what I believed because I was so sure I had it all worked out.

As Paul writes to Timothy, a young man, he tells him, 'Flee the evil desires of youth and pursue righteousness, faith, love and peace, along with those who call on the Lord out of a pure heart' (2 Timothy 2:22).

Paul doesn't state what all the evil desires of youth are, but one of them is the propensity to argue and quarrel—which is why Paul continues:

> Don't have anything to do with foolish and stupid arguments, because you know they produce quarrels. And the Lord's servant must not be quarrelsome but must be kind to everyone, able to teach, not resentful.
>
> — 2 TIMOTHY 2:23-24

Verse 22 makes it clear that being quarrelsome is evil, so in an exchange of words we might say that we're playing 'devil's advocate.' That declaration reveals who we're in league with! That's clearly not a good position for any Christian to take, and especially not a Christian leader.

Once again, we must be clear that Paul is not trying to train people to be mealy-mouthed and spineless. Leaders who let everything go and who don't have a razor-sharp interest in proclaiming and defending the truth are not going to scrub the church clean of the infectious disease that is false teaching. Church leaders must be able to spot and stand up to characters like Hymenaeus and Philetus. Leaders must have keen minds and be well trained theologically. But quarrelsome folks they must not be. You know the sort of person—they're utter pedants, ready to pick you up on every last detail.

Being people of the Word, where precision is such a necessary and good quality, is precisely why we need this helpful corrective. Taking a fastidious pedantry into things that don't matter leads to stupid arguments. Being pernickety about secondary issues and not being willing to ever let things go is foolish, and when all's said and done, it's not kind. But the Lord's servant (a description of the Christian leader) must be kind to everyone (verse 24).

I've seen young Christian leaders who are brilliant at handling God's Word, grind down church families with their pedantic accuracy born from a proud insistence on always being seen to be right on everything. In their pride they get irritated with the Christians under their care for not being more precise in their theology. What they don't realise is that the church family want to be loved. Be kind to them and then they'll be ready to be led. Quarrel with them over every last detail of every small issue and they'll get worn down and worn out.

What the young leader often fails to acknowledge is that they can win the argument and lose the person (or even lose the church family). If they were just to be a bit kinder in their engagement with those who oppose them, they might well win much more than the argument.

> Opponents must be gently instructed, in the hope that God will grant them repentance leading them to a knowledge of the truth, and that they will come to their senses and escape from the trap of the devil, who has taken them captive to do his will.
>
> — 2 TIMOTHY 2:25-26

Could Paul even have in mind here the likes of Hymenaeus and Philetus? We are to be kind even when encountering false teachers. In our discussion with them, our end game should be to see them repent of their false teaching and come back to the knowledge of the truth. I think of engagements I've had over the years with people in high office in the Church of England. To my shame, as a young man in leadership I did not approach those times with kindness. I was quarrelsome. My manner towards my detractors didn't commend the gospel of grace that I so passionately believed I was defending. In a more recent theological disagreement with a senior official in the Church of England I had this verse at the forefront of my mind. I trust I didn't go soft on the truth, but I did attempt to remain kind to the man I was in disagreement with. I wish I could write that he saw the light, came to repent and is now teaching the truth. That didn't happen, but I believe that in my desire to see the man repent and be freed from the trap of the devil, my manner matched the gospel I espouse. That's something that being quarrelsome and unkind would never have achieved.

Allan Chapple writes:

> The way I confront those who are promoting serious error must match the content of the truth I am seeking to uphold: grace-less behaviour brings no honour to the "God of all grace" (1 Peter 5:10) or the gospel of grace. So while I must be firm, I must also be gentle and kind, and while I should present clear arguments, I must not be an argumentative person (2 Timothy 2:23-26).[1]

John Newton, the slave trader who was gloriously converted by the amazing grace of God shared his concern about the way Christian leaders engage with others. In any encounter with others who had rejected the truth Newton suggested we see an opponent as someone who needs the gospel: 'he is a more proper object of your compassion than your anger' wrote Newton.[2] Newton's concern for lost souls was greater than his need to be seen to be right.

Having that attitude should enable us to flee the evil desire to win an argument and rather to be kind, and gently instruct those who oppose us. Be sure of this, quarrelling doesn't win people and it doesn't commend the gospel we say we stand for.

TRAIN LEADERS TO KNOW THE TIMES
WE LIVE IN

> But mark this: There will be terrible times in the last days.

— 2 TIMOTHY 3:1

My grandmother would often say to me, 'The world has become so evil, I'm sure the Lord will return soon. We must be in the last days.' As I've grown older I reckon my grandmother expressed what people of many generations have felt, a moral declension in society around us. I've felt it myself; British society does seem to be rapidly deteriorating. But while I have some sympathy with what my grandmother used to say, I also think she shared a common misunderstanding about two things. First that the world is steadily getting worse. Yes, there may be times when we appear to be moving further and further away from Christian values, but these things go in cycles. Societies from antiquity have been just as immoral as 21st-century Britain. You can't take a timeline of the history of the world and plot onto it a constant moral decline since the world began.

The second misunderstanding that my grandmother was verbalising concerned the biblical concept of the last days. She was right, we are in the last days, but she was also wrong. She understood the last days to be a few years before Jesus returned to wrap up history as we know it. But no, the last days have not come upon us in these last few decades of moral slippage.

John Stevens explains:

> Biblically, the "last days" is not a short period of time immediately preceding the physical return of the Lord Jesus to establish his kingdom on earth, but the whole era of salvation history from the moment of the ascension of the Lord Jesus and the outpouring of his Holy Spirit.[1]

In Acts 2:14-17, Peter explains that the pouring out of the Holy Spirit at Pentecost, as prophesied by Joel, signified the beginning of the last days. Here in chapter 3 of 2 Timothy, Paul wants Timothy to sit up and take note of what we can expect in the last days: 'But mark this: There will be terrible times in the last days' (2 Timothy 3:1).

Paul isn't writing this in an attempt to get Timothy's eschatology straight. Rather Paul is emphasising what it will be like to live in the entire period between Jesus' ascension and his final return. The whole period will terrible. That's not to say that there'll be nothing to rejoice in or enjoy in this life but Paul is spelling out that the last days will always be bad.

What a crucial thing to know. If church leaders have an over-optimistic view of the world we live in they'll soon find themselves disappointed and quite possibly crushed by the moral failure all around. Gospel workers must understand the times we're living in. The sad fact is that in the last days:

> People will be lovers of themselves, lovers of money, boastful, proud, abusive, disobedient to their parents, ungrateful, unholy, without love, unforgiving, slanderous, without self-control, brutal, not lovers of the good, treacherous, rash, conceited, lovers of pleasure rather than lovers of God—having a form of godliness but denying its power. Have nothing to do with such people.
>
> — 2 TIMOTHY 3:2-5

It's quite a list. What is perhaps most alarming is that this is not a description of out and out pagans, but the sort of people we'll find in the congregation on a Sunday; people who have 'a form of godliness but deny its power' (2 Timothy 3:5).

I've heard school teachers say, 'I love my job, it's the pupils I can't cope with.' Pastors can feel the same. 'I love preaching, it's the congregation that make life so trying.' It's not long before anyone in gospel ministry will find themselves encountering a good number of the characteristics listed in these verses, in those who claim to be Christians.

People are like this because of the Fall. The result of being sinful human beings is that the whole focus of life becomes self. Love of self is the antithesis of God's Law. In summarising the Law Jesus said we should love God and love our neighbour (Mark 12:29-31). What we read here is the polar opposite; in the last days, people will not love God or others, but they will love themselves (verse 2). That's the headline and then every trait listed in verses 2-5 can be traced back to self love.

- 'Lovers of money'—we love money because money gives us everything we want. Money satisfies self love, or at least that's what we think.
- 'Boastful' and 'proud'—because we love ourselves and think so highly of ourselves, we are proud and boast about ourselves and our achievements.
- 'Abusive'—when we love ourselves and think so highly of ourselves we feel quite at liberty to abuse others.
- 'Disobedient to their parents' and 'ungrateful'—why thank others for helping us if we think we're so great? When we love ourself, we think we deserve everything we're given. So we won't be thankful people, but ungrateful. What's more we'll be disobedient, arrogantly thinking we know better than everyone else, even our parents, who've been 'around the block' many more times than us.

We could work through the whole list and see that every character trait is an expression of disregard for God's Law to love the Lord and love our neighbour. This list demonstrates a complete reversal of the way we were designed to live. We were made to love God and love our neighbour, but in the last days people will love themselves.

K. Edward Copeland explains it like this:

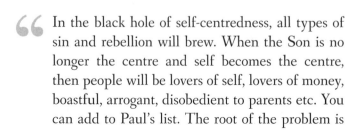

In the black hole of self-centredness, all types of sin and rebellion will brew. When the Son is no longer the centre and self becomes the centre, then people will be lovers of self, lovers of money, boastful, arrogant, disobedient to parents etc. You can add to Paul's list. The root of the problem is this inherent tendency in humanity to try to re-create reality so that we are the centre.

This root manifests itself in misdirected love. Instead of people loving God as God, they will love self to the point of deification.[2]

But as people deify themselves, don't assume that will result in total anarchy with everyone running around like cavemen! Self love is very clever. Love of self learns that in order to benefit self, there are times when it's necessary to be nice to others. Not for their benefit, but for ours. As a result the self-lover can appear to be outwardly 'godly' while inwardly being thoroughly selfish and self-centred. And so lovers of self have 'a form of godliness but [deny] its power' (2 Timothy 3:5).

That's what makes being a pastor so hard and so disappointing. Hard because people in the congregation look 'godly' as they live self-respecting, middle-class, religious lives. Their good lives lead us to assume they are Christians. How disappointing then, when those 'respectable and religious' people do something so utterly selfish and we discover they were never converted in the first place. On those occasions you feel such a fool to have been duped into thinking they were the real thing.

Gospel workers need to know the times we're living in. These are the last days. We must teach those in Christian leadership that there will be people in the congregation who will turn out to be lovers of themselves. Not just in the way that we are all forgiven sinners who struggle with selfish desires, but in that they actually deny the power of God to change them. Failure to grasp that will leave us completely bamboozled in gospel ministry.

1 9

TRAIN LEADERS TO HAVE NOTHING TO DO WITH CERTAIN PEOPLE

> Have nothing to do with such people.
>
> — 2 TIMOTHY 3:5

The ecclesiology of the reformers was gloriously clear when it came to making a distinction between the visible and the invisible church. The reformers taught that within any congregation there are those who are saved and those who are not. The visible church, those who gather together on a Sunday, will always be a mixture of saved and unsaved people. That distinction goes beyond the obviously unsaved people who call themselves inquirers. The visible church includes those who would speak of being committed Christians, but who are not saved. We must be clear of that, or we'll find ourselves easily hoodwinked by people who appear to be believers.

Paul warned Timothy about unbelievers in the visible church:

> People will be lovers of themselves ... having a

form of godliness but denying its power. Have nothing to do with such people. They are the kind who worm their way into homes and gain control over gullible women, who are loaded down with sins and are swayed by all kinds of evil desires, always learning but never able to come to a knowledge of the truth.

— 2 TIMOTHY 3:2, 5-7

We saw in the last chapter what people will be like 'in the last days.' The surprising conclusion is that these people are the very people who sit in church on a Sunday—they are part of the visible church. 'Some people pretend to fear the Lord, but use religion as a cloak for wrongdoing.'[1]

We must not be naive. Sadly, some people in the congregation have a form of godliness, but deny the power of the gospel which would change them from the inside out. They look like Christians on the outside, but haven't been changed deep down. It's one reason why gospel ministry can be so devastating. People who we thought were committed Christians do the most terrible things. The doctrine of sin tells me to expect this (everyone is fallen) and a right ecclesiology (the distinction between the visible and invisible church) prepares me for it too.

But we must also be aware that some self-serving religious people will attempt to make their way into positions of leadership. If they are 'successful' they will use and abuse their position in order to use and abuse others: 'They are the kind who worm their way into homes and gain control over gullible women, who are loaded down with sins and are swayed by all kinds of evil desires' (2 Timothy 3:6).

George Knight III helpfully points out that this is not a pejorative, misogynistic comment but a description of the particular situation.[2] Verse 6 is an illustration of how those who are not actually converted will use positions of church leadership to prey on the vulnerable.

The problem is, as we've sadly seen through recent high profile cases in the media, that leaders like this are skilfully adept at hiding their cruel and selfish actions. It's not easy to spot those who deny the power of God. In church on Sunday they have their Bibles open, they might attend midweek Bible study, and they can appear to be very knowledgeable about the Bible. But here's the thing about them—they are people who are 'always learning but never able to come to a knowledge of the truth' (2 Timothy 3:7). They're like a 'terrible two' from Moses' day: 'Just as Jannes and Jambres opposed Moses, so also these men oppose the truth. They are men of depraved minds, who, as far as the faith is concerned, are rejected' (2 Timothy 3:8).

That last definition of that gruesome twosome is critical. These are not genuinely born-again Christians who have fallen, they are unbelievers, 'as far as the faith is concerned, rejected.' It is about this sort of people that Paul says to Timothy, 'Have nothing to do with them' (2 Timothy 3:5).

Clearly we're not to avoid contact with all sinners. The Bible tells us to go and tell sinners the truth of the gospel. Jesus himself was the greatest friend of sinners, and we must befriend those in the congregation who are not yet born again. Paul is not giving instruction to avoid anyone who's not an obvious believer. In this very letter Paul has already even encouraged Timothy to engage with false teachers in the hope that they will come to their senses and repent. But, living in the last days as we do, we must be wise—some in the church are to be avoided. Lee Gatiss says:

These narcissistic charlatans who have the appearance of godliness but none of its reality are "corrupted in mind and disqualified regarding the faith" (verse 8). They are to be shunned and disassociated from, so that they cannot lead others astray.[3]

Paul is clear. Timothy is to have nothing to do with people like Jannes and Jambres. Authentic church leaders must disassociate from false leaders who are using their positions to feather their own nests at the expense of the salvation of others. We must learn to identify these 'lovers of self' so that we don't treat them as wayward believers who could be persuaded back to the truth, but have nothing to do with them.

Paul is training Timothy to be wise, and not to be naive. He has to realise, as we do, that not everyone in church, even those who have their Bibles open in church and in Bible studies, are actually born again. Paul is teaching Timothy to look out for people in the church family who, on the surface, and at first glance, appear to be the real thing. This is about having a clear doctrine of sin, a robust doctrine of the church and an awareness of the doctrine of the last days. These are things to teach future church leaders.

TRAIN LEADERS TO FOLLOW THOSE WHO ARE GODLY UNDER PRESSURE

> You, however, know all about my teaching, my way of life, my purpose, faith, patience, love, endurance ...

— 2 TIMOTHY 3:10

W ould you like to try this experiment?:

- Fill a glass full to the brim with any liquid.
- Stand the glass on a table.
- Knock the table as hard as you can with your fist.
- See what spills out of the glass.

You don't need to try the experiment, you already know the outcome. What spills out of the glass, is the liquid inside the glass. If the glass is full of water, water will come out. And here's the point: we're the same. When the knocks of life come our way, what comes out of us is what's inside us. Therefore if you want to meet the real person, observe them under pressure, when they get knocked by life.

When the heat is on, how many times have we heard—or indeed, found ourselves pleading—'This is not the real me. No, I'm normally very mild, self-controlled, measured, ...' (fill in the blank with your preferred adjective). The truth is that most of us are extremely adept at holding everything together in the normal run of life. We can present a public persona that is very acceptable, but when the pressure's on and we feel the heat, then the 'real me' comes spilling out. And please acknowledge that what comes out is the 'real me.' What comes out when we're knocked is what's inside. So, if you want to discover the real character of a church leader (or anyone for that matter), observe them under pressure.

Timothy had seen Paul in every kind of situation because Paul allowed Timothy into every aspect of his life: 'You, however, know all about my teaching, my way of life, my purpose, faith, patience, love, endurance' (2 Timothy 3:10).

We've seen already how Paul trained Timothy on the job and how invaluable that was for Timothy. Paul could repeatedly write in this letter, 'You know.' Here's another example of that, perhaps the best example of all. This verse makes it abundantly clear that Timothy had seen Paul from every angle, in many different situations.

It's a reminder that as we train the next generation of gospel leaders we must be ready to open up our whole lives to them and let them see what we're really like. Do life with them, and let them do life with us. But that makes verse 10 a phenomenal challenge. If a trainee followed me everywhere, and 'knew all about my way of life' (verse 10) they wouldn't need to ask anyone else what I'm like, they would know first-hand. And what would they see? A man full of faith? Patience? Love?

Endurance? What would they see when the heat was on? Someone enduring through 'persecutions and sufferings' (2 Timothy 3:11)? What a challenge.

Here is Paul inviting, even urging Timothy to make the comparison. It's as if Paul says, 'Compare my life to the life of those who are ungodly. Look at my way of life—what do you see? Having seen me at close quarters, what would you say was my purpose in life? When I was with tricky people did you see patience or did you see me lose my temper? In my dealings with others was I loving or selfish? And crucially, through trials and persecutions, did you see me endure, or did you see me throw in the towel when the going got tough?'

Paul was confident that as Timothy thought carefully about every aspect of Paul's life, he would conclude that Paul was no fraud. That should really challenge all of us. But again, this is not primarily to challenge those of us who train others (even though it should do that) but to give Timothy a benchmark of genuine Christian leadership. Paul wanted Timothy to see precisely the kind of leader he should follow, and by implication the kind of leader he should become in order to be a trainer of others.

These few verses are remarkably challenging, but Paul's detractors could have a field day at this point. This could so easily appear to be an unattractive boastful claim from the apostle, a proud self assessment. 'Look at me—I am very impressive don't you think.' The end of verse 11 should dispel any such thought. Listing the significant persecutions he endured, Paul writes,

> You, however, know ... what kinds of things happened to me in Antioch, Iconium and Lystra,

the persecutions I endured. Yet the Lord rescued me from all of them.

— 2 TIMOTHY 3:10-11

Paul is not boasting of his own remarkable achievements. He gives the glory to God. It was the Lord who rescued him from those most dangerous and challenging situations. It was the Lord who enabled Paul to endure.

That's wonderfully encouraging, but it must not be mis-applied. This is not a promise of deliverance from any and every difficult situation we may face in gospel ministry, indeed it can't be. We know Paul is about to be executed for his faith in Christ (2 Timothy 4:6). What Paul is doing here is boasting in the Lord. His remarkable claim to have lived a godly life through all manner of hardships is the Lord's work. The Lord rescued Paul from all manner of trials. And Timothy needs to know that the Lord is with his people through suffering, because 'everyone who wants to live a godly life in Christ Jesus will be persecuted' (2 Timothy 3:12).

Timothy, and any gospel leader (come to that, any Christian), needs to know that living a godly life will result in persecution. We live in the last days and people love darkness more than light. Persecution is not an unusual part of being a Christian, it goes hand in glove with living a godly life. So what an encouragement for Timothy to recollect how the Lord rescued Paul from all his significant trials around Asia Minor.

But again, the primary aim is that Timothy should know what the life of an authentic Christian leader looks like, in comparison to evil men who have a form of godliness but deny its power.

> ... everyone who wants to live a godly life in Christ Jesus will be persecuted, while evildoers and impostors will go from bad to worse, deceiving and being deceived.

> — 2 TIMOTHY 3:12-13

Paul had suffered and been persecuted but through it all he endured. When the knocks of life came, he didn't give up. A resolute, indefatigable, tenacious, persistence spilled out of Paul whenever he faced a hard time and he remained faithful. Timothy had witnessed that. In every situation Timothy had seen Paul was full of faith, patience and love. In one word he was 'godly.' Paul didn't just have a form of godliness (2 Timothy 3:5). Paul's godliness was genuine and came with power, the power to live a godly life, even in the most trying of circumstances. Paul *was* a leader to follow, because when he was knocked, godliness spilled out!

21

TRAIN LEADERS NEVER TO DEPART FROM THE SCRIPTURES

> But as for you, continue in what you have learned and have become convinced of ...
>
> — 2 TIMOTHY 3:14

In my study hangs a picture of the faculty and students from my last year at theological college. Captured in that snapshot are not only smiles for the camera but also scores of hopes and dreams for the future. Many of us are just weeks away from leaving behind us our residential theological education, to embark on a lifetime of full-time paid gospel ministry. That photograph arouses a number of different emotions for me. There are many happy memories, some significant sadness and a very big dollop of reality. As my eye scans the top line of students, I see Harry. On the second row Geoffrey is beaming from ear to ear. On the front row, Frank sits proud and upright with his arms crossed. The thing is, Harry, Geoffrey and Frank are all dead now. They've been taken from us through tragedy in the form of a debilitating degenerative disease, a terrible accident, and a past that became too unbearable to live with. I rejoice that those guys all knew the gospel and so I have confidence that they're now with the Lord. But still, it saddens me to think they're no longer with us.

That said, I feel an even greater heartache when I look at some others in the photograph. It wouldn't be right for me to tell you the names of those others. Seeing them sitting there, smiling broadly, leaves me feeling great anguish because since the shutter clicked to capture that moment, they have given up believing the Bible. It's a reality check because at college we were united in the gospel. We enjoyed attempting to get to the bottom of great theological truths. The Bible was our rule. We were determined to teach the Word in the power of the Spirit to change the world, or if not change the world, we had ambitions to influence England for good and for the gospel. But now, more than one or two who shared my gospel convictions don't any longer believe the Bible as the fully inspired, infallible and inerrant Word of God. I met one of my college cohort at an event a few years back. Not having seen each other for 25 years we brought each other up to speed with where we lived and how our families were doing. The conversation turned to the struggles of life and gospel ministry. I said something about the spiritual battle we're all in and the wily schemes of the evil one trying to derail us. He replied, 'Oh, don't tell me you still believe in a literal devil. I didn't think anyone believed in that nonsense any more. I moved on from that fairytale years ago.' As the conversation developed it became evident that he didn't any longer believe the Bible as his final authority in all things.

Sadly, many 'evangelicals' give up on the Bible. It is crucial therefore that in training future gospel leaders we give them deep convictions about the Bible as the Word of God. Then we must urge them never to move from those convictions. Paul wrote to Timothy, 'But as for you, continue in what you have learned and have become convinced of' (2 Timothy 3:14).

The contrast here is with 'evildoers and imposters [who] go from bad to worse, deceiving and being deceived' (verse 13). There will be people who will lose their way. I take it these are the people who are the subject of the first part of chapter 3, those who have a form of godliness but who deny its power (2 Timothy 3:5). If that's right then these people are church people, religious types, imposters in church congregations who masquerade as genuine Christian people. In contrast to them, there's one sure way to be sure to stay on the straight and narrow, and that's to stick to the Scriptures:

> But as for you, continue in what you have learned and have become convinced of, because you know those from whom you learned it, and how from infancy you have known the Holy Scriptures, which are able to make you wise for salvation through faith in Christ Jesus.

— 2 TIMOTHY 3:14-16

It's very important to understand what's going on here. A cursory reading could lead us to conclude that verses 14 and 15 entirely hark back to Timothy's childhood. There clearly is a reference back to his earliest years, but I'm not convinced that Paul is telling Timothy to continue in what he learnt from his grandmother Lois and mother Eunice (2 Timothy 1:5). Yes, his Granny and Mum were believers, but there's nothing in this letter to suggest that Timothy became a follower of Jesus through those two god-fearing women. It's more likely that Timothy became a Christian through Paul, who was Timothy's spiritual father (2 Timothy 1:2 and 1 Timothy 1:2). Timothy learnt Christ from Paul, and the immediate context in chapter 3 is of Paul reminding Timothy all about his (Paul's) way of life (verse 10). Therefore it seems most consistent to understand Paul to be the one from whom Timothy learned Christ. This is then a call for Timothy not to depart from the faith that he learned from Paul.

Now we must be careful here. If we plucked this verse out of context and sent it to a good friend in a greetings card, it could be read to suggest that everyone should continue in the faith they were first taught, but that can't be right. What if we were taught wrong things when we first became a Christian? What if we'd been taught the Bible by a theologically liberal Christian? Or a Jehovah's Witness? This is not a verse telling everyone who reads it to carry on in the faith they were first given. As always with the Bible we must understand this verse in its original context. The reason Paul can tell Timothy to continue in what he learned is because Timothy learned it from Paul, and Paul was an apostle (2 Timothy 1:1). Therefore what Timothy learned is authentic apostolic Christianity, New Testament Christianity. Verse 14 is then an exhortation to continue in the apostolic faith, or we could say, the New Testament Scriptures. Then Paul adds, 'and how from infancy you have known the Holy Scriptures' (2 Timothy 3:15).

The Holy Scriptures here are what we now call the Old Testament Scriptures, the Scriptures that grandmother Lois and Timothy's mother Eunice had regularly read to Timothy when he was growing up.

Put that all together and we have the New Testament (verse 14) and the Old Testament (verse 15). In short, Paul is saying, 'Timothy, do not depart from the Bible.' Continue in apostolic biblical Christianity. Don't depart from the Bible; don't be one of those who sits smiling in front of a camera with hopes and dreams of a faithful gospel ministry, only, in years to come, to have given up on the Bible as your final authority.

Like Paul, we must implant in potential leaders the primacy of the authority of Scripture, and urge them never to depart from the Bible as their final rule.

22

TRAIN LEADERS TO BELIEVE THE BIBLE WILL FULLY EQUIP THEM FOR MINISTRY

> " All Scripture is God-breathed and is useful for teaching, rebuking, correcting and training in righteousness, so that the servant of God may be thoroughly equipped for every good work.

> — 2 TIMOTHY 3:16-17

Anyone who's been involved in gospel ministry for more than five minutes will know the temptation to look for a magic formula for growth and success. But as a former colleague would often say to me, 'There is no silver bullet.'

I used to lead a lunchtime gospel work in London's West End. We saw modest growth in the numbers attending, but we were surrounded by tens of thousands of people who poured into the West End every day for work, entertainment and 'retail therapy.' The vast majority of them were lost, without God and without hope in the world. With an evangelistic concern and a desire to see the ministry grow, I longed for more to attend our lunchtime meetings, so I would regularly find myself wondering if we'd make a breakthrough if the music was better, or the seating was arranged differently, or the sandwiches we served were tastier!

In gospel leadership we'll often be tempted to look for a solution beyond the Bible. Of course there's nothing wrong with trying to get the music right and the ambiance of the room pleasant and to be sure to serve delicious food. But at the end of the day we need just one thing to lead the church, and that is the Bible. That's what Paul tells Timothy here:

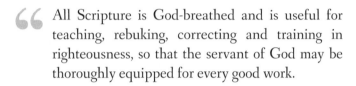 All Scripture is God-breathed and is useful for teaching, rebuking, correcting and training in righteousness, so that the servant of God may be thoroughly equipped for every good work.

— 2 TIMOTHY 3:16-17

The 'servant of God' here is the church leader. With the Bible in hand, the church leader is thoroughly equipped for *every* good work. The Bible equips me for evangelism and church growth and pastoral counselling and discipleship and church council decisions and matters of discipline and church polity and, well, for everything. What's more, the Bible is not just adequate for the task, it leaves me thoroughly equipped for the task.

I am one of those people who wants to be sure to cover every base in every situation I find myself in. So, for example, whenever we go on holiday I over-pack. I take thick jumpers when going to the Mediterranean in the summer, just in case the temperature takes an unexpected dive! I take more books to read than I can possible get through on a ten-day vacation just in case we get stranded at the airport. I take more foreign currency than I intend to spend just in case all our luggage is diverted to outer Mongolia. You might be thinking I need serious help with my pathological pessimism! But putting my psychological profiling to one side, you get the point: I like to cover every base. But when preparing for a day of gospel ministry I can travel light. The only provision I need to cover every possible turn of events in gospel ministry is to have my Bible to hand. The Scriptures equip me as a gospel minister for everything that might come my way in that day.

Paul began this chapter urging Timothy to make note that we are living in the last days. He warned that the last days will be terrible days. The chapter ends with Paul telling Timothy that all he needs is the Bible. The Bible gives us everything we need even when we come up against stubborn, selfish godlessness (3:1-5), and opposition to the truth (3:8), and depraved minds (3:8), and persecution (3:11-12), and evil imposters in the church (3:13), and deception (3:13). And that's because 'All Scripture is God-breathed and is useful for teaching, rebuking, correcting and training in righteousness' (2 Timothy 3:16).

Teaching the Bible is how we stand against false teachers: it rebukes and corrects. Teaching the Bible is how people are turned from their selfish love of themselves. The Bible is all we need in evangelism, as it is able to make people wise for salvation in Christ Jesus (2 Timothy 3:15). The Bible rebukes and corrects error. The Bible teaches and trains in how to live a righteous life. The Bible is all the pastor needs to be thoroughly equipped for every good work we might be called to do.

But though I've had that conviction for many years, yet still I am tempted to look for that illusive silver bullet. I learned this verse by heart shortly after I became a Christian and still I find myself wondering if the 'magic formula' for church growth is to be found somewhere else.

> Paul instructs Timothy to devote himself to preaching the Word (2 Timothy 4:2), precisely because that Word makes the man of God "adequate, equipped for every good work" (2 Timothy 3:17). Timothy didn't need the latest rhetorical techniques, business practices, or creative ministry models based on captivating metaphors. He simply needed to be guided, governed, and geared by the Word of God.[1]

In gospel ministry there will often be a temptation to look to other things to grow the church or guide us in making tough decisions, or tackle false teachers. We must be sure we not only teach a sound doctrine of Scripture from verse 16, but also that we train ourselves and future leaders to believe in the sufficiency of Scripture.

23

TRAIN LEADERS TO PREACH THE WORD

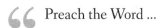 Preach the Word ...

— 2 TIMOTHY 4:2

There are many things to occupy a gospel minister's time. Every day there are people to see, meetings to attend, schedules to rota, administration to deal with, phone calls to take, emails to send. But there is one thing that the church leader must be about, and that is preaching the Word. You might expect to hear that from a conservative evangelical stable, but this is not the specific emphasis of an esoteric church group. As Paul begins to draw his letter to a close he lays down a magnificent charge:

In the presence of God and of Christ Jesus, who will judge the living and the dead, and in view of his appearing and his kingdom, I give you this charge ...

— 2 TIMOTHY 4:1

Those are weighty words—the stakes could not be higher. First, consider that we are in the presence of greatness, in the presence of God the Father and Christ Jesus the Son. Second, acknowledge his majestic authority in being the one who will judge everyone who has ever walked planet earth, the living and the dead. Third, keep in view the day when Jesus Christ will return to this earth to appear in all his glorious majesty. Fourth, know that there will be a day when he will usher in his everlasting kingdom. Timothy, have these immense thoughts at the forefront of your mind as I give you this charge.

Any one of these awesome statements would be enough to make Timothy sit bolt upright and take note. God is present, the God who will judge all mankind. The God who will one day come crashing into time to bring to a close history as we know it. The God whose kingdom will be established forevermore as all rivals are eternally restrained. With such a compelling and intense curtain-raiser what might we expect Paul to write next? Of course, we know what Paul writes next, but do you see what a surprise it is given the introduction? 'Preach the Word.' Is that it? Do we really need such a prologue for what appears to be such an undistinguished task? Well, yes we do, lest we think that preaching the Word *is* an undistinguished task. Preaching the Word is *the* task that Timothy must give himself to. Preaching the Word is the task that all church leaders must be committed to. Be sure, preaching is much more than addressing a group of Christian people from a pulpit. We should proclaim the Word of God to large gatherings of people, but also in small groups and one to one. And of course we should preach the Word both to Christians and unbelievers alike. One way and another, we must preach the Word. This we must stress when training the next generation of gospel workers, because all manner of other urgent and important matters will distract gospel workers from the task of proclaiming the Word.

But what will it mean to preach the Word and why should this be the task?

1. PREACH THE WORD, BECAUSE WE'RE IN THE LAST DAYS

At the beginning of chapter 3 Paul stressed that Timothy must expect terrible times because we live in the last days. The sinfulness of human beings will be frighteningly evident. Dominated by self love, people will live selfish, self-centred and self-absorbed lives. Even those who appear to be religious will take advantage of vulnerable people. The answer to living in these terrible times is to preach the Word. As we stated in the last chapter, the Scriptures thoroughly equip the church leader for the task before us until Christ returns. Preaching the Word is the antidote to self love. Preaching the Word is the way to break through granite-like hearts, hearts that will never be changed by religion or religiosity.

2. PREACH THE WORD, NOT ANYTHING ELSE

It might seem obvious that it is the Word that we must preach yet in the last chapter we noted the constant temptation to look for a magic bullet. There's often a temptation to believe that there's something else we need to do that will bring us the breathtaking breakthrough we long for in gospel ministry. But even if we have the conviction, and the presence of mind, to continue to believe that preaching is what we're to be about, there is a further temptation, and that is to preach our own ideas. I'm not thinking here of the preacher who doesn't ever refer to the Bible—that type of preacher is clearly not preaching the Word. I'm thinking about preachers who have the Bible open but then import their own ideas. It's a danger for the academic intellectual. It's a danger for the brilliant orator. It's a danger for anyone.

3. PREACH THE WORD, EVEN WHEN IT'S UNPOPULAR

Just a few weeks into my first curacy, at a weekly supervision session, my training incumbent, David Wheaton, said to me, 'Paul, there are only two occasions when it's appropriate to preach the Word.' I don't mind telling you that my heart sank. For a brief moment I began to wonder if I'd been unwise in taking on a training post with David. Then he completed the sentence, 'There are only two occasions when it's appropriate to preach the Word, in season and out of season. When it's convenient and when it's not. When it suits you and when it doesn't. When it's popular and when it isn't.' That's what Paul says here: 'Preach the word; be prepared in season and out of season' (2 Timothy 4:2).

I'm in the wonderful situation where the vast majority of the church family thank me for preaching the Word, even when it's a hard-hitting challenge. But faithful gospel ministry means being ready to preach the same Word in churches where people don't like the message and won't thank us. We must have the courage of our convictions to teach that same Word when we have unbelievers before us and when we expect it won't be popular. Preach the Word when people might be rude to you as they say good-bye at the door. Preach the Word when folk pepper your inbox with aggressive emails. Proclaim the Word when your hearers will complain to the Bishop and cause all sorts of trouble for you. Preach the Word. The bottom line is that sinful people don't want to hear the Word. Many will search for, and find, teachers to say the things they want to hear, but we must not be one of those teachers.

> For the time will come when people will not put up with sound doctrine. Instead, to suit their own desires, they will gather around them a great number of teachers to say what their itching ears want to hear. They will turn their ears away from the truth and turn aside to myths.
>
> — 2 TIMOTHY 4:3-4

We must impress upon future leaders the need to preach the Word (and not our own ideas) because the Word is so counter-cultural and challenges the accepted norms of the day. Preach the Word even when it will question the largely unchallenged evangelical idols of education and wealth creation and careerism. Preach the Word about the uniqueness of Christ and the reality of judgement and the confinements of sexuality and sexual practice. It won't be popular because there'll be plenty around who'll say what people want to hear and sadly many of those false teachers will occupy church pulpits.

4. PREACH THE TONE OF THE WORD

All of us broadly fall into one of two categories. We are either primarily an encourager or predominately a rebuker. It's either our predilection to exhort or to challenge. That might sound so binary as to be unhelpful, but because we're not perfect we will all swing towards one extreme or the other. As a result, there's a potential problem: if we tend to be largely a rebuker, the church family we lead will eventually be worn down by a constant barrage of challenges and rebukes. On the other hand, if we are more the encouraging type, we'll shy away from reproaching and correcting the error and sin in the church family, and while they'll love us for all our encouragements, a diet of only positive affirmation is like an unhealthy regimen of only sweet foods. In the long run it won't do a church family any good. However, if we preach the Word faithfully, we'll not only say true things, but we'll say them in the tone they are written. So Paul writes, 'Preach the word; be prepared in season and out of season; correct, rebuke and encourage' (2 Timothy 4:2).

We should preach the Word in these different tones and styles because different passages (and books) of the Bible have been written in these varied ways. It's what Paul stated back at the end of chapter 3: 'All Scripture is God-breathed and is useful for teaching, rebuking, correcting and training in righteousness' (2 Timothy 3:16).

As Scripture will teach, rebuke and correct, so faithful preaching of the Word will be a rich variety of correcting and rebuking and encouraging. I've had to work hard on this because I naturally err towards challenge and rebuke. So I can take a passage that was written to encourage and exhort and leave people feeling 'beaten up,' but if I do that, while I might be saying true things, I am not preaching the Word faithfully.

Here's why it's so helpful to systematically preach through different books of the Bible. If we take note of the tone of the books and passages we're preaching, over time, the church family will receive the precise balance of rebuke, correction, training and encouragement they need.

5. PREACH THE WORD, PATIENTLY AND CAREFULLY

In view of all that we've just considered it's no wonder that Paul writes, 'Preach the word; be prepared in season and out of season; correct, rebuke and encourage—with great patience and careful instruction' (2 Timothy 4:2).

It takes careful instruction to be sure to handle the Bible accurately. When preparing to teach the Bible we not only have to ask what does this passage say, but also how does it say it. But in addition to tone we also do well to think about genre. As I come to the Scriptures I'll encounter poetry, apocalyptic literature, epistle, narrative, history, parable. Gloriously, the Lord in his sovereign kindness has given us many kinds of literature appropriate for every occasion. Careful handling of the Bible will see me change my presentation style to fit the genre of literature I'm engaging with. When we modify our preaching/teaching style to fit the literature before us we become even more faithful in handling the Scriptures and most importantly, we have more chance of connecting with the people we teach. And that's the point of all this. As we've already seen, in these last days people don't want to hear the Word of God, rather they want to hear what they want to hear. They want to find people to deal with their problem of paraesthesia of the hearing and equilibrium organ—that's the medical term for itching ears! Don't be an ear scratcher. Rather be someone who teaches the Word of God with great patience and careful instruction. Note the word 'for' at the beginning of verse 3:

 Preach the word; be prepared in season and out of season; correct, rebuke and encourage—with great patience and careful instruction. For the time will

come when people will not put up with sound
doctrine. Instead, to suit their own desires, they
will gather around them a great number of
teachers to say what their itching ears want to
hear.

— 2 TIMOTHY 4:2-3

Preaching must be done with great care. It is a precision
activity. We handle Scripture faithfully when we cut straight
and true through a Bible passage. It is the Word of God that is
powerful to change people, not our ideas, so our careful
instruction will be necessary in order to get through to those
who don't want to hear God's Word.

Furthermore, we need to take great care when preaching
and teaching God's Word because we will be dealing with
issues that profoundly affect people's lives. Divorce and
remarriage, career choice, how to spend time and money, issues
of sexuality and of course the ultimate issues of the eternal
salvation of men and women and boys and girls. The stakes are
high and extreme care is required. Care that we don't only tell
people what they want to hear, or tell them untrue things that
no-one should hear.

Take care but also be patient. The charge is to preach the
Word with great patience. People don't change overnight. Look
honestly at yourself—you didn't change overnight! You
probably still don't change quickly. Word ministry is a slow
ministry. Jesus' parables in Mark 4 tell us that. We have to be
patient. There's a balance here: in order for our preaching to
have edge and bite we must believe that every sermon could be
utterly life-changing. But if that's all we believe we'll be
regularly disappointed when we don't see dramatic change.

Then comes the temptation to shout louder, or to rely on funnier stories (for me, never mind funnier, just funny would be a start!). We can even learn what buttons to press that will induce a response. That's very dangerous and can flow from an impatience and an insecurity that is desperate to see a response. To counter that we must believe that Word ministry takes time; great patience is required in any Bible teaching ministry.

This is deliberately the longest chapter in this book, because in 2 Timothy 4:2 we come to the high point of the letter. Preaching the Word is the great and primary duty of the gospel worker and church leader. That's evident by looking at the way Paul introduces the charge. The next generation of gospel leaders must be left in no doubt that their chief objective must be to preach the Word, carefully, patiently, faithfully, continually.

24

TRAIN LEADERS TO DO THE WORK OF THE EVANGELIST

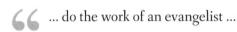

66 ... do the work of an evangelist ...

— 2 TIMOTHY 4:5

S heena stated it brilliantly, 'The church family will knock on your door asking for your help through a pastoral crisis, or to lead their Bible study, or to chair another meeting, but you won't ever have unbelievers knocking on your door asking you how to become a Christian. So unless you make evangelism a priority you'll never do it.' It's a brilliant little statement perfectly encapsulating a constant tension in Christian leadership. Even leaders who are the most enthusiastic evangelists can find a God-given zeal for the lost swamped by the demands of the church family and church polity. But the church must always be looking outwards and the church leader sets the tone for a church. So, Timothy must 'do the work of an evangelist' (2 Timothy 4:5).

I love this phrase for two reasons. First, because the church leader is to do the work of the evangelist whether or not they feel they have the spiritual gift of evangelism. I'm sure I'm not the only one to have heard church leaders describe themselves as 'a pastor and not an evangelist.' We understand the sentiment behind such a statement. We may even have said it, or thought it, ourselves. There are many really fine gospel workers who don't feel especially equipped or able when it comes to that great task of taking the glorious gospel to unbelievers. And in a world where people want their itching ears to be scratched by people who will say what they want to hear, the evangelistic task is never easy. So, what a temptation for the leader to focus on teaching the flock to the exclusion of any personal evangelism. But here Paul doesn't tell Timothy to 'fan into flame' his gift of evangelism, he tells Timothy to do the work of the evangelist whether he has that particular spiritual gift or not.

Second, I love this phrase because Paul doesn't tell Timothy to simply do evangelism. A general misconception about evangelists is that they're the people who tell people about Jesus. They go door knocking, engage in street evangelism, start up conversations on the train, run Christianity Explored groups, preach at guest services and always have another story of a person who they recently led to Christ. Incidentally, writing a list like that can be the precursor to a pejorative comment. But no, I'm not denigrating anyone who has a go at any of the activities listed above or any person who is wonderfully gifted in speaking about Jesus and leading people to Christ. The church needs as many evangelists as it can get. Oh, that we were all as bold and fruitful as the sort of person I've just described. But with that caveat sincerely in place, allow me to broaden our horizons when it comes to the work of the evangelist. The evangelist is to do more than speak to people about Jesus. The gift of the evangelist is given to the church to equip every Christian in the church family to do evangelism. That understanding widens the role of the evangelist from being the one who does evangelism to the one who equips every Christian in the task of evangelism. In Ephesians chapter 4 Paul writes, 'So Christ himself gave the apostles, the prophets, the evangelists, the pastors and teachers, to equip his people for works of service' (Ephesians 4:11-12).

The evangelist is listed as one of the gifts given to the church by the risen, ascended and exalted Christ. The four Word gifts named here—apostles, prophets, evangelists and pastor/teachers—are given so that the church is equipped to serve and so build up the body of Christ (Ephesians 4:12). Question: how then does an evangelist equip God's people for works of service? Answer: by teaching them the work of evangelism.

So 'the work of the evangelist' that Timothy is charged to do, is more than telling Timothy to do evangelism. Yes, as a church leader Timothy should make time to meet, befriend and talk to unbelievers about the gospel of Jesus Christ, but it's more than that. The work of the evangelist includes training and equipping the church family in the great commission to go and make disciples. Doing the work of the evangelist is one aspect of the task of preaching the Word. As we faithfully teach the Bible we will inevitably be training, correcting and encouraging people to tell others about Jesus.

Subsumed into this call to do the work of the evangelist are three matters for Timothy and every church leader to be about.

1. BE PERSONALLY EVANGELISTIC

While the task of the evangelist is greater than 'doing personal evangelism' it cannot be less than that. Precisely because the evangelist is to train others to do evangelism, they must themselves be engaged in that task. If they're not, at least two things will happen. First they'll be called hypocrites by the church family. There's never a place in gospel leadership to tell people to do something that we ourselves are not doing. The Christian life must be modelled by Christian leaders. This is true in every area of life, and not least of all when it comes to gospel proclamation. It's difficult telling people about Jesus. We will be rejected. At times evangelism involves putting precious relationships on the line. So when we're asking others to do evangelism, if we're not doing it ourselves, we'll be accused of hypocrisy and that'll be reason enough for people to reject our teaching, even if what we're saying is good and right.

Second, we need to be about evangelism to keep our teaching relevant and real. If we're not personally engaging with unbelievers we'll be out of touch and not be engaging with the issues in the world today.

The gospel never changes. The answer to the greatest need of humanity is always the same, but the questions people are asking change from decade to decade. So the way we present the unchanging truth of the gospel needs to be subtly adapted. If church leaders last found themselves seriously engaged in evangelism 20 years ago, they'll be out of touch. Further, if we're not personally engaging with unbelievers we can soon begin to think that evangelism is easy. Then we might present evangelistic techniques as cast-iron guarantees to win arguments and make converts.

Regularly spending time with unbelievers is a constant reminder of how hard it is to start gospel conversations, keep them on track, and bring Jesus into the heart of the encounter. Gospel workers must be personally evangelistic.

2. BE TRAINING THE CHURCH FAMILY

We've seen from Ephesians 4 that training Christians is a key aspect of the work of the evangelist. Future gospel leaders must be taught how to do this, whether it be laying on evangelism training courses, preaching in such a way that equips the church family in evangelism, or using evangelistic courses (like Christianity Explored) not only to reach out to unbelievers, but to train regular members of the church family in evangelism.

Part of my earliest evangelism training was in being part of a beach mission team and then helping at a university mission. Being part of teams who were led by gifted evangelists taught me so much. The team leaders of those missions deliberately taught their teams a whole range of skills, and we gleaned a whole range of skills and wisdom from simply watching the evangelist in action.

The work of the evangelist is to train others in evangelism and gospel leaders need to do this for those in their charge.

3. SET AN EVANGELISTIC CULTURE IN THE CHURCH FAMILY

Doing personal evangelism and training the church family in it should go a long way towards creating a culture of outreach in the church. But we can further do that by employing a whole raft of ideas, big and small.

We can ensure the church programme has regular high quality and low-cringe evangelistic events, regularly scheduling guest services and having an evangelistic course running every term. These things say something powerful to the church family about the importance of evangelism. That can be further reinforced by making every Sunday gathering outsider-friendly.

That doesn't mean holding 'seeker-services' every week, or bolting onto the end of every sermon the ABC of how to become a Christian. Services can be made to feel accessible to outsiders by welcoming newcomers from the front and using language that doesn't exclude people.

We can also help to show how important evangelism is in an informal way. When people ask to meet up with me I sometimes explain that I'm not available at a certain time because that's when I play tennis with my unbelieving friend— you'll have to believe me that that's not just an excuse to avoid another Christian meeting. At church family prayer meetings when we pray for our non-Christian friends and neighbours, I might tell the church family who I'll be inviting to an upcoming guest service. All this says something to the church family about why we're here. It creates an evangelistic culture.

The church can so easily forget that it is meant to be a lifeboat to save perishing souls. It is the task of the church leader to keep evangelism high on the agenda, so we must train the next generation of gospel workers to do the work of an evangelist.

25

TRAIN LEADERS TO CARRY OUT EVERY MINISTRY DUTY

> ... discharge all the duties of your ministry.
>
> — 2 TIMOTHY 4:5

Gospel ministry is one of those 'careers' (and there are many of them) where the job is never finished. No matter how much is achieved in a day, a week, a month or a year, there's always more that could be done. There are more people to visit, more books to read, more one to one Bible studies to lead, more intercessions to pray, more unbelievers who need to hear the gospel. I'll stop the list there before this chapter becomes extremely long and overwhelming! No-one in gospel ministry need wake up in the morning wondering how they're going to fill their diary. No-one in gospel ministry should ever feel bored with nothing to do. And there lies the problem with this verse—to discharge all the duties of ministry, if misunderstood, could lead the gospel worker to an early coronary or an emotional break down. Sadly, that's been a reality for far too many gospel workers.[1] The job has overwhelmed some to the serious detriment of their health and even to early promotion to glory! But be sure of this, Paul is not telling Timothy to work himself into the ground by working every hour that God sends, in an attempt to do every possible task that everybody suggests is part of ministry. We must read this verse in its context. The end of this magnificent charge is a call to be sure not to avoid the tough elements of gospel work that can be so dispiriting.

We've seen that the preeminent enterprise for the church leader must be the preaching and teaching of God's Word. That must be done faithfully, even when it will go down like a brick in a swimming pool—something that will often be the case, as Paul has just reminded Timothy. Many people don't want to hear the gospel. Their ears are burning to hear things other than the gospel. Then Paul writes, 'But you, keep your head in all situations, endure hardship, do the work of an evangelist, discharge all the duties of your ministry' (2 Timothy 4:5).

In the last days we'll always be surrounded by people who don't want to hear the gospel and we'll be disappointed by those who desert the gospel when the going gets tough. When that happens, Timothy must keep his wits about him, be clear-thinking. It will mean enduring hardship, remembering that suffering is to be expected in gospel ministry. It means doing the work of evangelism and not timidly ducking the responsibilities of church leadership. To discharge *all* the duties of his ministry will mean paying attention to *all* the things Paul has already laid out in this letter.

We considered earlier in the book how Timothy has been so worn down by false teachers and by desertion that he will be sorely tempted to avoid the battles of gospel ministry. He'll be tempted to keep his head down, rather than keeping his head in every situation. At times he'll want to avoid hardship, and as a result, *not* fulfil *all* the duties of his ministry; he has the duty of preaching the Word in season and out of season, and the duty of contending for the gospel when it would be so much easier to just work hard in pastoring the flock. He'll think about avoiding hardships, rather than enduring them. Timothy will be sorely tempted to reduce his ministry to only pastoring the Christians in Ephesus rather than doing all the other things this letter has encouraged him to do.

As Paul urges Timothy to discharge all the duties of his ministry he's not telling him to attend to every conceivable demand of a church family. He's not asking him to be enslaved by the countless requirements imposed by everyone who has an opinion on how the pastor should fill his time. Paul is saying, don't shirk away from the things you really must be doing: enduring hardship, doing evangelism, fighting the fight.

In training the next generation of gospel leaders it's vital that we give them a clear grasp of what is expected of them by God in the Scriptures. That way they'll be able to assess and evaluate the expectations of the congregation. Equally they'll know what really is expected of them by the God who judges all and so discharge *all* the (God-given) duties of their ministry.

26

TRAIN LEADERS TO EVALUATE
MINISTRY IN THE LIGHT OF THE END

> ... there is in store for me the crown of righteousness, which the Lord, the righteous Judge, will award to me on that day—and not only to me, but also to all who have longed for his appearing.

— 2 TIMOTHY 4:8

What are the longings of your heart? What do you daydream about? You know those moments when your mind wanders and you catch yourself far away. Where are you —on a beach or playing sport? What are you doing—relaxing or eating good food? Who are you with—your significant other or the significant other you don't yet have? The longings of our heart are very telling. I regularly have to 'take captive every thought to make it obedient to Christ' (2 Corinthians 10:5). Too often my daydreams expose and reveal how my heart longs for a perfect hassle-free retirement with my wife. I long for a retirement when I imagine enjoying a peaceful easy feeling all day long.

There are all sorts of problems with that idol in my heart, but for now let me state just three. The longings of my heart don't extend far enough, aren't nearly ambitious enough and they're not with the right person. By glorious contrast the longings of the apostle Paul's heart are spot on. Paul longs for the appearing of Christ (2 Timothy 4:8). He is looking further ahead than retirement. He longs for Jesus' return. And Paul is longing to be with Jesus. On that day everything really will be well. It's a great longing to have, not least of all because it is guaranteed to be realised and when it comes to pass it won't disappoint. And here's the thing, the longings of our heart, influence how we shape the present.

Paul is near to death: 'For I am already being poured out like a drink offering, and the time for my departure is near' (2 Timothy 4:6). Nevertheless, he's not freaked out by the thought, because he's embraced the gospel. The gospel of Christ alone prepares us for that day. As Paul nears the end of life he's able to reflect on his life and say, 'I have fought the good fight, I have finished the race, I have kept the faith' (2 Timothy 4:7).

We considered these verses in chapter 1. They are central to the whole letter (and to this book). Paul is facing death with a contentment not only because of the gospel, but because he has trained the next generation of gospel leaders. I won't cover that ground again. For now see these words in the context of Paul's longings. Paul wanted more than anything to meet Jesus and be with Jesus. He longed for his appearing. He knew that on that glorious day of Christ's return the most precious award would be bestowed upon him: 'Now there is in store for me the crown of righteousness, which the Lord, the righteous Judge, will award to me on that day' (2 Timothy 4:8). What a reward! It makes the Queen's New Year Honours list look decisively second rate. Paul will be given a crown of righteousness awarded by none other than the King of Kings, the greatest honour ever.

It is that future—honoured by the Lord, in the Lord's presence, with the Lord forever—that kept Paul fighting (the good fight), running (the race) and labouring (to keep the faith). Paul had his eyes on the prize. His heart's desire was to be with Jesus, the One who was everything to him. He would rather be with Jesus than have anything on earth because he knew being with Jesus was better by far. On the other hand, Paul so loved Jesus that he was willing to stay on earth and work hard in gospel ministry if that's what the Lord wanted of him (Philippians 1:21-24). But this is not unique to Paul. Note the phrase in verse 8, 'and not only to me':

> Now there is in store for me the crown of righteousness, which the Lord, the righteous Judge, will award to me on that day—*and not only to me*[1], but also to all who have longed for his appearing.

> — 2 TIMOTHY 4:8

Paul is not the only person on the Lord's New Creation Honours list. All who have longed for the glorious appearing of Jesus will be presented with *that* crown. And it is that crown, and that future with Jesus, that will keep us going in the Christian life and through all the significant trials of gospel ministry.

- When tempted to be ashamed of the gospel because

it will cause me suffering, a longing for that day will keep me faithful.

- When thinking of modifying the gospel to be more palatable, a longing for that day will stop me from doing so.
- When disappointed by the desertion of those who have previously stood with us in gospel ministry, a longing for that day will pick me up.
- When worn down by the hardship and sacrifice of gospel ministry, a longing for that day will give me the resolve to keep going.
- When confronted by false teaching, a longing for that day will keep me battling.
- When surrounded by wicked self-centred people, a longing for that day will keep me sane.
- When overwhelmed by the demands of preaching the gospel to people who don't want to hear it, a longing for that day will keep me discharging all ministry duties.

When a longing for Christ's appearing is our heart's desire, then we will keep going and not give up. In Christ we have a future that is substantial and certain, unlike the castles in the air that we construct in our make-believe daydreams. Our fantasy worlds won't ever satisfy the desires of our hearts and they certainly won't keep us going in gospel ministry. But longing to be with Jesus and longing for his return will motivate us so that we'll reach the end of our lives having fought the good fight, finished the race and kept the faith. That's a longing to put before every gospel worker.

TRAIN LEADERS BY BEING VULNERABLE WITH THEM

 Do your best to come to me quickly ...

— 2 TIMOTHY 4:9

Our world wants leaders who are strong and resilient, men and women who appear immune from the struggles we 'lesser mortals' have to endure. A Prime Minister coughs and splutters their way through a conference speech and it's a mark of weakness that is derided. A Presidential candidate on the punishing schedule of an election trail cannot be seen to be tired or ill. An Emperor who isn't the picture of health is a liability to the nation. That same need for leaders to present themselves as superhuman can easily be adopted in the church. But it's a most unhelpful model of Christian leadership and Jesus certainly didn't embrace it. He was the *servant* leader whose weakness was strength, so in training the next generation of gospel leaders we must not try to hide our vulnerability. More than that, we need to be secure enough to highlight it. Paul did that very thing here at the end of his letter to Timothy:

> Do your best to come to me quickly, for Demas, because he loved this world, has deserted me and has gone to Thessalonica. Crescens has gone to Galatia, and Titus to Dalmatia. Only Luke is with me. Get Mark and bring him with you, because he is helpful to me in my ministry. I sent Tychicus to Ephesus. When you come, bring the cloak that I left with Carpus at Troas, and my scrolls, especially the parchments. Alexander the metalworker did me a great deal of harm.
>
> — 2 TIMOTHY 4:9-14

Paul was quite clearly an exceptionally resilient man—the way he suffered for the gospel was extraordinary. The list of trials he recalls in 2 Corinthians 11:23-29 is astonishing: incarcerated, beaten up, flogged to within an inch of his life, shipwrecked and in danger from highway robbers, working exceptionally hard without sleep or food or water. When I consider that list I reckon I'd have caved in after the first spell in prison, but Paul kept going. Yet he doesn't present himself as a self-sufficient Rambo type 'he-man.' Paul is not ashamed to be vulnerable with Timothy.

First, he needs others in ministry. 'Timothy, do your best to come to me quickly.' 'Only Luke is with me.' 'Get Mark and bring him with you because he's helpful to me in my ministry.' Even the great apostle needed people to help him in gospel ministry. So we must not pretend that we can go it alone; we must not present a pattern of gospel ministry that would suggest that we can cope without the help of others. We need to model the importance of working in teams and the huge value of forming strong gospel friendships and partnerships.

Second, Paul expresses his pain. 'Alexander the metalworker did me a great deal of harm' (verse 14). The 'strong man' approach to leadership does not allow the leader to express any sense of distress caused by another. Someone crosses a President and the President dismisses them, showing the world that, in his eyes, everyone is thoroughly dispensable. He doesn't need anyone, and he uses a press conference to trash the individual in question and give the impression that the incident has not bothered him in the slightest. But Paul is quite different—he openly admits that Alexander the metalworker caused him great harm.

Third, Paul admits to his loneliness in ministry: 'At my first defence, no one came to my support, but everyone deserted me. May it not be held against them' (2 Timothy 4:16).

Gospel leadership can feel like a very lonely place sometimes. Paul clearly had a good number of faithful friends around. A number of them are listed at the end of this letter: Timothy, Crescens, Titus, Luke, Mark, Tychicus, Priscilla, Aquila, Erastus, Trophimus, Eubulus, Pudens, Linus, Claudia, Onesiphorus and his family. Paul had friends, loyal gospel friends, but he felt utterly deserted at his first trial. This wasn't the kind of gospel desertion we saw from Demas (2 Timothy 4:10). Demas deserted the gospel out of love for the world. As Paul went before the court in Rome, Plummer suggests, 'among all the Christians in Rome there was not one who would stand at his side in court either to speak on his behalf, or to advise him in the conduct of his case, or to support him by a demonstration of sympathy.'[1]

That hurt, but as we've seen before, Paul quickly put the other side of the case by stating that he was not all alone. 'The Lord stood at my side' (2 Timothy 4:17). That's an important word of testimony for Timothy to read should he ever face such a horrid situation of abandonment. But as wonderful as the Lord's faithful presence is, Paul still expressed the loneliness he felt in that time of desertion.

It's very easy to read about Paul's ministry and think that he powered on through every painful trial like a macho superhero. But that selective reading is extremely unhelpful. It leaves us feeling thoroughly inadequate whenever we feel the pain, hurt and loneliness of gospel ministry and whenever we feel the need of gospel friends to partner alongside us. Paul's readiness to be vulnerable here is very real. It teaches Timothy that it's quite normal to experience the agony of loneliness in gospel ministry. For that reason, we too, must be prepared to be vulnerable when training future gospel ministers.

TRAIN LEADERS TO READ BOOKS

> When you come, bring ... my scrolls, especially
> the parchment.
>
> — 2 TIMOTHY 4:13

Many years ago I met with a young man who was part of the church I was involved with at the time. We met for coffee but I can't, for the life of me, recall the reason we arranged to get together. However, as we talked it became very evident that he was a very well thought-out Christian. He had been raised in a Christian home and converted at university. He'd always attended churches where the Bible was at the heart and centre of the ministry. The type of churches he'd been a part of were churches where the staple biblical diet was a systematic working through of whole books of the Bible. They were churches where careful exposition and relevant application would be prized and appreciated by the church family. So, it was no wonder that this young man was wise and mature—he'd been well taught.

But I've met many people who've attended good Bible teaching churches who have not been as thoroughly theologically rounded as this fellow, so I began to ask myself what it was about him that made him so clear thinking and well-rounded. As we spoke it became evident that he was committed to setting aside a substantial chunk of time at the beginning of each day to read the Bible and pray. That, I was sure, was another factor in his being well-rounded. But then, in the course of our conversation I discovered that he was a reader. He loved books, he read Christian books, he always had a book on the go and apart from setting aside a chunk of time each day to read, he would carry a book with him and dip into it when he found himself with a few spare minutes, waiting for a bus or before a meeting began. I put two and two together and concluded that it was his devotion to reading good Christian books that had supplemented the good Bible teaching he had received from the churches he had been involved in.

This young man was wise, mature, disciplined and serious about following Jesus. He had a terrific attitude of heart and a humility that resulted in him wanting to learn and put into practice all that he heard from God's Word. These qualities were unquestionably part of why he was such an impressive disciple. But I'm convinced the books made a difference too. There's something about being in the habit of reading good Christian books that is invaluable.

You might expect all those in gospel ministry to be readers, but there are many in leadership who have given up the discipline of reading. It's easy to let it slip. As we've considered more than once, gospel ministry brings so many demands every day. Carving out time to read can appear to be a luxury we cannot afford or an expendable pastime we can ditch. But I suggest that reading is indispensable.

As we move into the last section of Paul's letter to Timothy, we're given a wonderful little insight into Paul's 'needs.' Looking forward to a forthcoming visit from Timothy Paul writes, 'When you come, bring the cloak that I left with Carpus at Troas, and my scrolls, especially the parchments' (2 Timothy 4:13).

I love Paul's request that Timothy retrieve and then deliver his cloak. Paul wasn't a materialist, but he also certainly wasn't one of those super-spiritual types who talk as if they don't need anything physical. Winter was coming (2 Timothy 4:21) and he would soon have to deal with the cold. He needed to keep warm, he needed his cloak. But then there was something else he wanted, his books. I can do no better than to quote Spurgeon here:

 We do not know what the books were about, and we can only form some guess as to what the parchments were. Paul had a few books which were left, perhaps wrapped up in the cloak, and Timothy was to be careful to bring them. Even an apostle must read. Some of our very ultra Calvinistic brethren think that a minister who reads books and studies his sermon must be a very deplorable specimen of a preacher. A man who comes up into the pulpit, professes to take his text on the spot, and talks any quantity of nonsense, is the idol of many. If he will speak without premeditation, or pretend to do so, and never produce what they call a dish of dead men's brains —oh! that is the preacher. How rebuked are they by the apostle! He is inspired, and yet he wants books! He has been preaching at least for thirty years, and yet he wants books! He had seen the Lord, and yet he wants books! He had had a wider experience than most men, and yet he wants books! He had been caught up into the third heaven, and had heard things which it was unlawful for men to utter, yet he wants books! He had written the major part of the New Testament, and yet he wants books! The apostle says to Timothy and so he says to every preacher, 'Give thyself unto reading.' The man who never reads will never be read; he who never quotes will never be quoted. He who will not use the thoughts of other men's brains, proves that he has no brains of his own. Brethren, what is true of ministers is true of all our people. You need to read.[1]

Let's be sure we impress upon those we train, that reading good Christian books is not an activity to be sacrificed on the altar of the demands of gospel ministry.

29

TRAIN LEADERS ABOUT CHRISTIAN ASSURANCE

<blockquote>

The Lord will rescue me from every evil attack and will bring me safely to his heavenly kingdom.

— 2 TIMOTHY 4:18

</blockquote>

The Christian doctrine of assurance is deeply comforting but at times, perplexing; on the one hand pastorally wonderfully reassuring, and on the other, unhelpfully falsely assuring.

Many Christians need to be better assured of their salvation as a faithful expression of God's love and true reflection of Christ's saving work. A more thorough and deep heartfelt assurance would release some Christians to be sold out for Jesus, freeing them from feeling the need to put some of their eggs into a worldly basket. But on the other hand, a misuse of the glorious truth of assurance can be pastorally disastrous, giving wayward Christians license to indulge in lifestyles that will cause them great spiritual harm. The doctrine of assurance has also left many a believer perplexed when they see other Christians fall away.

The tensions and complexities of such an important theological issue are immense. Christian leaders need to rigorously grapple with these issues in order to be prepared and able to present the nuances of this doctrine carefully and appropriately when pastoring others. Clearly this is not a book to equip anyone for that (it's not thick enough to begin with!), but in this chapter we will begin to grapple with the importance for Christian leaders to have a clear grasp of Christian assurance when it comes to their own gospel ministry.

These last verses are so much more than 'personal instructions' or 'personal remarks' as some translations label them. Paul returns here to two of the key themes in this letter, two of the big issues that are so distressing in Christian leadership, the issues of desertion and opposition. To do this he lays before Timothy the final 'terrible two of 2 Timothy.' Demas and Alexander are the gruesome twosome in this section.

First Demas deserted Paul: 'Do your best to come to me quickly, for Demas, because he loved this world, has deserted me and has gone to Thessalonica. Crescens has gone to Galatia, and Titus to Dalmatia' (2 Timothy 4:9-10).

In chapter 27 we considered how lonely Paul felt in gospel ministry, a pain which was exacerbated by Demas. Crescens had zoomed off to what we now call Turkey, Titus had made his was to the eastern coast of the Adriatic sea. Chances are they both left Paul in the cause of the gospel, but Demas's foray to Greece, was for no reason other than that he loved the world. He deserted the gospel, and his departure resulted in Paul feeling vulnerable and was a key reason behind Paul wanting Timothy to join him as soon as he could. When confronted with this kind of disloyalty to the gospel, we need others around us.

Second, we discover that Alexander the metalworker had been doing more than manufacturing iron goods; he'd been making trouble by opposing the inspired gospel. He was dead set against Paul's message in a way that caused Paul considerable harm:

> Alexander the metalworker did me a great deal of harm. The Lord will repay him for what he has done. You too should be on your guard against him, because he strongly opposed our message.
>
> — 2 TIMOTHY 4:14-15

In telling Timothy about the double trouble that came from Demas and Alexander, Paul is telling was him that he can expect desertion and opposition in gospel ministry. But as we saw in chapter 27, Paul knew the Lord's presence and strengthening through those trials, and it was God's ever-present help in trouble that enabled Paul to carry on the urgent task of proclaiming the gospel to the Gentiles. The Lord gave Paul all he needed so that he could discharge all the duties of his ministry (2 Timothy 4:5):

> At my first defence, no one came to my support, but everyone deserted me. May it not be held against them. But the Lord stood at my side and gave me strength, so that through me the message might be fully proclaimed and all the Gentiles might hear it.
>
> — 2 TIMOTHY 4:16-17

As we've noted in a previous chapter this letter does not give us the false assurance that the Lord will always keep us physically safe. After all, Paul is about to die for the faith. But we are given the assurance that even when the great hardships of desertion and opposition raise their ugly heads, we should not conclude that we're doing something wrong, and we should not begin to wonder if God has deserted us. Even when we're downhearted and feel lonely because of desertion and opposition, the Lord stands by us and strengthens us to enable us to fully proclaim the gospel.

All that is crucial reinforcement for Timothy to know about Christian leadership, but there's something new here too. Paul writes, 'And I was delivered from the lion's mouth. The Lord will rescue me from every evil attack and will bring me safely to his heavenly kingdom. To him be glory for ever and ever. Amen' (2 Timothy 4:17-18).

Paul can testify to being delivered from the schemes of Satan and he has assurance that he'll be kept until he is safely in God's heavenly kingdom. There's a terrific balance here of both present rescue and eschatological salvation. Paul's autobiography is so extraordinary (remember that list in 2 Corinthians 11:23-29) that he doesn't need to embellish an event, or use hyperbole in his writing, or adopt any histrionics to make his story sound exciting. When he writes here of being delivered from the lion's mouth, we can assume he is describing an event where it was very nearly the end for him.

Elsewhere Satan is described as being like a roaring lion (1 Peter 5:8). Here Paul paints a graphic picture of being inches away from Satan gobbling him up, but the Lord delivered him. Once again, this is not a promise of physical deliverance for all gospel workers for all time. Paul was about to die for his faith in

Christ, but I do believe this incident is testimony to an occasion when the Lord delivered Paul from a near-death experience.

What we do know is that we have an enemy who loves devouring Christians as tasty morsels in his rebellious fight against Almighty God. And faithful Christian leaders are an especially delicious snack for the devil—he loves nothing more than to bring down an effective gospel worker. Yet, listen to the assurance here: Satan cannot do anything beyond the Lord's will. We can be sure that the Lord will not allow Satan to thwart his purposes. That should leave us feeling very safe.

But again, being safe in the shadow of the Lord isn't a guarantee that we'll reach a ripe old age and 'enjoy' a peaceful death, slipping away in our sleep. That wasn't Paul's experience or the experience of many of God's faithful servants (Hebrews 11). The Lord's keeping, however, is an assurance that he will keep us safely going with him until we are in his heavenly kingdom (2 Timothy 4:18).

Gospel leaders need to understand and trust this balance, this tension if you will, knowing that the Lord can and often does deliver his people, but there are times when it is the Lord's sovereign will for a life to end. We should not give in to the false assurance that we could never face what some might describe as an 'untimely death.'

What we do have here is confidence in the ultimate future deliverance of complete salvation for eternity, not because we will manfully keep going, but because the Lord is committed to bringing us safely to his heavenly kingdom. We need that understanding of Christian assurance if we're to press on when facing desertion and significant opposition. He will keep me until the end.

We must train leaders to understand Christian assurance.

Gospel ministry is tough, and hard work, and even dangerous sometimes, but the Lord will keep us going to the end, and take us safely to his heavenly kingdom.

30

TRAIN LEADERS

 The Lord be with your spirit. Grace be with you.

— 2 TIMOTHY 4:22

"**F**inally! Many Christian preachers use the word "finally" then appear to forget they have said it, but this chapter really is the last. So *finally,* let me urge you to make training leaders something that you will be committed to doing for the rest of your days, whether you're the lead pastor of a church, a full-time paid gospel worker, heading up an area of ministry, or leading a small group in your local congregation. When you close the last page of this book will you be committed to identifying and then training at least one person who could do your job after you?

The first step to making that commitment is to be convinced that training the next generation of gospel workers is not an optional extra. That takes us back to where this book began, so let me again project you forward to that most sacred moment in anyone's life—your deathbed. Read again those words of Paul as he felt his life ebbing away:

> For I am already being poured out like a drink offering, and the time for my departure is near. I have fought the good fight, I have finished the race, I have kept the faith. Now there is in store for me the crown of righteousness, which the Lord, the righteous Judge, will award to me on that day—and not only to me, but also to all who have longed for his appearing.

— 2 TIMOTHY 4:6-8

As you read these words, be assured that the glorious gospel gives complete assurance of salvation, the free unmerited gift of God that is by grace alone, through Christ alone and effected by faith alone. As you picture yourself on your deathbed, drink in that reassuring good news. But then, assured of salvation, as you lie there, think back through your life. Believe me, you will do that. Then imagine the relief of being able to say (as much as any of us can), 'I have fought the good fight, I have finished the race, I have kept the faith.' What a satisfying experience to know that largely you've given the greatest part of your life and your greatest energy and effort to the greatest mission known to mankind. And then, what a glorious feeling to know that you have trained the next generation who will give themselves to the task of serving Jesus and his gospel and, in turn, train others to do the same. Feel the relief of knowing that work has been done and the gospel legacy you have left.

Facing death Paul knew that he had kept the faith. By the grace of God he had remained true to the gospel himself and he had trained Timothy. As he commissioned Timothy, Paul had guarded the gospel by faithfully giving it away to another who would faithfully give it to others. Paul could 'rest assured.'

To be committed to training leaders we need to be convinced that gospel succession is not an optional extra that can legitimately appear some way down our 'to do' list. Once we are convinced of that, then we need to shape our diaries to reflect that priority. Create time. Cut out of your schedule other worthy things. Be ruthless. Have 'training leaders' as an item in your prayer diary. Pray daily, or at least regularly, about identifying, training and deploying future leaders—pray for those you are training.

That said, before I wrap things up, a word to those who feel exhausted in gospel ministry. I hope you've been inspired by this walk through 2 Timothy, but I can imagine this exhortation may well leave you feeling overwhelmed. You're convinced of the need to train leaders. You want to do it. But you're already flagging and these chapters feel like an additional 30 things to add to your already extensive 'must do' list. If you are feeling inspired but daunted by the task and not knowing where to start, let me encourage you to start small. Find one or two people who love the Lord, love his Word and love his people. Begin by sharing your life with them. Be honest with them about the joys and struggles of ministry. Tell them about your priorities, your concerns, your work. As you deliberately share life and ministry with others, they will 'catch hold of' many of the things listed in this book. If you're worn out already, don't set up a 30 week training course for a bunch of prospective gospel ministers, do what you can with the one or two you have. Invite them along to things you'd be doing anyway and then discuss with them how and why you do what you do. Along the way you can refer back to the chapters in this book and be sure to drop into conversation the content of the different chapters.

So finally (there's that word again), having taken you to your deathbed (twice now), allow me to project you just 10 years ahead. Imagine that from today, every current evangelical Christian leader would make an investment to identify and then train a future gospel worker. If we all did that just once in the next 10 years then ... well, you can do the math. In just 10 years we would double the number of trained and deployed gospel workers in this land. That's an exciting prospect as it is. But understand the current climate and it's all the more pressing and thrilling.

In the denomination I am a part of, in the next 10 years, around 2000 ordained stipendiary ministers will retire—25% of the current church leadership. There are nowhere near enough people currently training to fill those roles so there is an urgent need. But there's also a fantastic opportunity. Many of those leaders retiring in the next decade are not evangelicals. Churches that have never had the gospel clearly and faithfully preached to them will be crying out for people to lead them. We could fill those vacancies with 'Timothys'! How exciting is that? Not to mention the opportunities to plant more churches and of course send people all over the world in cross-cultural mission.

Training one person in the next 10 years is not beyond any gospel worker. For many current gospel workers, in a decade, we could replicate that training several times over. Then allow me to project you another 10 years forward. If all those newly trained leaders trained one new leader, and all the current leaders repeated the exercise again, in 20 years from now we would be 'leadership equipped' to achieve something quite spectacular in this land. Especially if we trained the next generation to be hard workers who were ready to make sacrifices for the gospel like the soldier, the athlete and the farmer. We'd have an army of leaders who would be prepared to strain every ligament to labour hard in handling the Word of God correctly. We'd have leaders ready to sacrificially go anywhere to please their commanding officer. We'd have a resilient bunch of workers who'd be ready to keep going through the disappointments of desertion and all the exhausting battles of dealing with false teachers. We'd have trained people to unashamedly stand for, and suffer for the apostolic gospel. We'd find the Word of God preached when it was convenient and when it wasn't, in the pulpits of this land, in small group Bible studies and in coffee shops as people met to study the Bible one-to-one. We'd have leaders who were committed to doing the work of the evangelist, leading in personal evangelism, creating an evangelistic church culture and training whole church families to be better equipped to share Jesus with others.

It is of course the Lord's prerogative to do what he would with our efforts. But living in a nation where millions are drifting to a lost eternity and where the church is in decline, I don't want to float along, drifting with the current. I want to at least attempt to swim against the tide, so that when I reach the end of my life I can look back and think that I had made a good attempt at changing the direction of travel in this nation. In short, I want to die having tried to change things, and one key way to effect gospel change is to train leaders. Will you commit to playing your part in doing that?

In all your gospel ministry and especially as you seek to train the next generation of gospel workers, 'The Lord be with your spirit. Grace be with you' (2 Timothy 4:22).

NOTES

1. THE PRIORITY OF TRAINING LEADERS

1. Chris Green, Commentary, Oak Hill College, Winter 2011/12
2. John Stott, *The Message of 2 Timothy*, p114

3. TRAIN LEADERS TO RELY UPON THE LORD

1. Alfred Plummer, *The Pastoral Epistles*, page 314

5. TRAIN LEADERS THE AUTHENTIC GOSPEL FOR WHICH THEY MUST SUFFER

1. 'We see [the] integrating centre in the purpose of the Father, which is that all should give the highest honour to the Son (John 5:22-23; Phil 2:9-11). We see it in the work of the Spirit, all of which is aimed at glorifying the Son (John 16:14). We see it in the scriptures, which are all about the Lord Jesus. We see it in the gospel, which is the gospel of Christ for the word of Christ. Its subject is the worth of Christ: it is "the gospel of the glory of Christ" (2 Cor 4:4, NASB). It presents him as the Father's unique Son, the Lord of all, the Saviour of the world. So the gospel is the word of Christ about the worth of Christ. The gospel also centres on what he has done for us: it is the word of Christ about the work of Christ. It is "the message of the cross" because it concerns Christ crucified. It also proclaims his resurrection from the dead and exaltation to heavenly rule as Lord of all. [.....] The Bible makes is very clear that everything in God's word and work focuses on his Son. If we are to do God's work in God's way, the Lord Jesus himself must therefore be the focus and centre of our ministries.' Allan Chapple, *Ministry Under the Microscope : The What, Why, and How of Christian Ministry*, p130-131.

6. TRAIN LEADERS HOW TO GUARD THE GOSPEL

1. John Stott, *The Message of 2 Timothy*, p. 47
2. C K Barrett, *The Pastoral Epistles, The New Clarendon Bible*, Oxford University Press, 1963, p. 97

8. TRAIN LEADERS ON THE JOB

1. Ken Smith, *With Him*, pages 48 and 49
2. Richard Bewes, *Equipped To Serve*, p71

13. TRAIN LEADERS TO WORK HARD IN THE WORD

1. Lee Gatiss, *Fight Valiantly! Contending for the faith in the Bible and in the Church of England*, p85

15. TRAIN LEADERS TO BELIEVE IN THE DOCTRINE OF GOD'S ELECT

1. John Stott, *The message of 2 Timothy*, page 70

17. TRAIN LEADERS NOT TO BE QUARRELSOME

1. Allan Chapple, *Ministry Under The Microscope*, Latimer, p.48
2. John Newton, *The Works of John Newton*, vol. 1, Banner of Truth, Edinburgh, 2015 (originally published 1839), p113

18. TRAIN LEADERS TO KNOW THE TIMES WE LIVE IN

1. John Stevens, *Knowing our times*, p.13
2. K. Edward Copeland, *Entrusted with the gospel*, ed by DA Carson, page 93

19. TRAIN LEADERS TO HAVE NOTHING TO
DO WITH CERTAIN PEOPLE

1. David Gooding and John Lennox, *The Bible and Ethics*, p88
2. George W Knight III, *The Pastoral Epistles: A Commentary on the Greek Text*, Carlisle:Paternoster, 1992, p433-434
3. Lee Gatiss, *Fight Valiantly: Contending for the faith in the Bible and in the Church of England*, p88

22. TRAIN LEADERS TO BELIEVE THE BIBLE
WILL FULLY EQUIP THEM FOR MINISTRY

1. Mark Dever & Paul Alexander, *The Deliberate Church: Building Your Ministry on the Gospel*, Crossway, 2005, p.21

25. TRAIN LEADERS TO CARRY OUT EVERY
MINISTRY DUTY

1. If you are unhelpfully feeling the pressure it might be worth putting this book down and picking up Christopher Ash's excellent, *Zeal Without Burnout* published by The Good Book Company

26. TRAIN LEADERS TO EVALUATE MINISTRY
IN THE LIGHT OF THE END

1. Emphasis mine

27. TRAIN LEADERS BY BEING VULNERABLE
WITH THEM

1. A. Plummer, *The Pastoral Epistles* (The Expositor's Bible) p. 420

28. TRAIN LEADERS TO READ BOOKS

1. Charles H Spurgeon, *Paul—His Cloak and His Books* A Sermon (No. 542), Delivered on Sunday Morning, November 29th, 1863, At the Metropolitan Tabernacle, Newington